MS-DOS®
QuickStart

Developed by Que® Corporation

Text and graphics pages developed by
David W. Solomon and Lois Sherman

Que® Corporation
Carmel, Indiana

MS-DOS Quickstart

Library of Congress Catalog No.: 88-61791

ISBN 0-88022-388-X

92 91 90   8 7 6 5 4

Interpretation of the printing code: the rightmost double-digit number is the year of the book's printing; the rightmost single-digit number, the number of the book's printing. For example, a printing code of 89-4 shows that the fourth printing of the book occurred in 1989.

This book can be used with DOS versions 3.0 and later.

Publishing Director

David P. Ewing

Product Director

Lois Sherman

Acquisitions Editor

Terrie Lynn Solomon

Editors

Lois Sherman
Cheri Robinson

Technical Editor

Bob Breedlove

Production

William Hartman
Jennifer Matthews
Dennis Sheehan

Proofreaders

Peter Tocco
Carolyn A. Spitler

Indexer

Sherry Massey

Composed in Garamond by
H<small>ARTMA</small>N
Publishing

Page Design by

William Hartman, Hartman Publishing
Cheri Robinson

Acknowledgments

Que Corporation thanks the following individuals for their contributions to this book:

David Solomon, for his technical expertise and talent for making DOS easy to understand, and for the many long days and nights he spent seeing this porject completed.

Lois Sherman, for her developmental work on this book, including refining the original outline, editing the text, and creating many of the graphics spreads.

Bill Hartman, of Hartman Publishing, for his design contributions, for his willingness to make numerous modifications and additions to the text, and for the many extra hours he put into completing this project.

Bob Breedlove, for his expert technical review of the text.

Tim Stanley, for his technical assistance, especially for his simple explanations of complex ideas.

Jeff Booher, for his cheerfully provided technical assistance.

Joanetta Hendel, for her editorial assistance in preparing the appendixes.

Stacey Beheler, for her administrative assistance to the editors working on this book.

The Que Production department, for their skillful paste-up and photographic work and their efforts during the final production stages of this book.

Trademark acknowledgments

Que Corporation has made every attempt to supply trademark information about company names, products, and services mentioned in this book. Trademarks indicated below were derived from various sources. Que Corporation cannot attest to the accuracy of this information.

Andrew Tobias' Managing Your Money is a registered trademark of MECA (Micro Education Corporation of America).

Apple is a registered trademark of Apple Computer, Inc.

AT&T is a registered trademark and UNIX is a trademark of American Telephone & Telegraph Company.

Atari is a registered trademark of Atari Corporation.

Commodore is a registered trademark of Commodore Electronics Limited.

COMPAQ is a registered trademark of COMPAQ Computer Corporation.

dBASE IV is a trademark of Ashton-Tate Corporation.

EPSON is a registered trademark of Epson Corporation.

First Publisher is a trademark of Software Publishing Corporation.

Freelance, Lotus, 1-2-3, and Symphony are registered trademarks of Lotus Development Corporation.

IBM is a registered trademark and PS/2 is a trademark of International Business Machines Corporation.

Leading Edge is a registered trademark of Leading Edge Products, Inc.

Microsoft and MS-DOS are registered trademarks of Microsoft Corporation.

PageMaker is a registered trademark of Aldus Corporation.

Quattro is a registered trademark of Borland International, Inc.

Reflex: The Analyst is a trademark of Borland/Analytica, Inc.

SideKick Plus is a registered trademark of Borland International, Inc.

Smart is a copyright of Innovative Software.

SuperCalc is a registered trademark of Computer Associates International, Inc.

Tandy 1000 is a registered trademark of Tandy Corporation.

Ventura Publisher is a registered trademark of Ventura Software, Inc.

WANG is a registered trademark of Wang Laboratories, Inc.

WordPerfect is a registered trademark of WordPerfect Corporation.

WordStar is a registered trademark of MicroPro International Corporation.

XyWrite III is a trademark of XyQuest, Inc.

Zenith is a registered trademark of Zenith Electronics Corp.

Contents

3 Booting the Computer

4 Using DOS Commands

Contents

7   Copying and Deleting Files

8   Protecting Data

Contents

9 Special Commands

10 Batch Files

Appendix A

Appendix B

Appendix C

Index

Conventions Used in This Book

Certain conventions are used throughout the text and graphics of
MS-DOS QuickStart to help you better understand the book.

In the Text

This book uses a symbolic form to describe command syntax. When
you enter a command, you substitute real values for the symbolic
name. Examples show you commands that you can enter exactly as
shown.

DOS commands can have various forms that are correct. For example,
the syntax for the DIR command looks like this if you use symbolic
names:

> **DIR** *d:filename.ext /W/P*

DIR is the command name. The *d:filename.ext* is a symbolic example
of a disk drive name and a file name. A real command would have
actual values instead of symbols.

Some parts of a command are mandatory—required information
needed by MS-DOS. Other command parts are optional. For the DIR
command example, the **DIR** is mandatory. The rest of the command,
d:filename.ext /W/P, is optional. When you enter only the mandatory
command elements, DOS in many cases uses already-established
values for the optional parts.

You can type upper- or lowercase letters in commands. DOS reads both as uppercase letters. You must type the syntax samples shown in this book letter-for-letter, but you can ignore case. Items shown in lowercase letters are variables. You type in the appropriate information for the items shown in lowercase.

In the example, the lowercase *d:* identifies the disk drive the command will use for its action. Replace the *d:* with A:, B:, or C:. The *filename.ext* stands for the name of a file, including its extension.

Spaces separate some parts of the command line. The slash separates other parts. The separators, or delimiters, are important to DOS because they help DOS break the command apart.

For example, typing **DIR A:** is correct; **DIRA:** is not.

Text that you are to type is displayed in **boldface**. Screen displays appear in this `special typeface`.

In the Graphics

Keys are shown as they appear on the keyboard. Red lines emphasize the most important areas of the graphic illustrations.

To the Reader

MS-DOS QuickStart uses a new approach to introduce the fundamental concepts of DOS to beginning users. Throughout the book, each DOS topic is presented in two- to six-page text spreads, followed by graphics spreads. The graphics illustrate the topic discussed on the text pages.

This book describes the connection between personal computer hardware and the disk operating system and explains all the most frequently used DOS commands. In addition, *MS-DOS QuickStart* contains chapters that cover the topics of hierarchical directory organization and batch files. After you become familiar with DOS's commands and features, you can use the graphics in *MS-DOS QuickStart* for reference.

MS-DOS QuickStart is your guide to becoming comfortable using DOS on your personal computer!

Introduction

MS-DOS QuickStart is a step forward in the evolution of how a book can be organized and structured. The entire book is built around two- to six-page *spreads*. Each spread, of either text or graphics, presents an overview of a topic. The graphics spreads illustrate the concepts.

Spreads are connected to form chapters, which in turn make up the complete book. Titles of all the chapters in the book are listed down the right side of each spread. Topics in the current chapter are listed across the top of the page. Highlighted rectangles pick out the current chapter and topic. The rectangles work like a set of crosshairs, zeroing in on the major subject and the specific topic covered in that spread.

How Does *MS-DOS QuickStart* Do Its Job?

Using this book is a lot like using a map. First, to grasp all the main elements, you look at the aerial view. Then you look closer to find street names and the place where you are heading. The visual structure of this book, like a map, offers you quick access to information.

The key to using this book is to use the text and graphics for what each does best. The graphics convey overviews, relationships, and connections. Text supplies essential information that the graphics can't, provides comments on what you see, and describes abstract ideas.

Each spread in this book contains highlighted rectangles that show your exact location. The side rectangle shows which chapter you are in. The top rectangle shows which topic of the chapter you are in. To see everything that is covered in any chapter, scan across the topics at the top of the page.

Each rectangle moves as you progress through the text. If you flip through the pages quickly, you can see the side rectangle moving up or down and the top rectangle moving left or right. By watching the rectangles, you always can see where you are in this book.

What Is MS-DOS?

MS-DOS (or to most PC users, just *DOS*) is the world's most popular computer *D*isk *O*perating *S*ystem. DOS is a set of programs that form a foundation for you and your programs to work effectively with your computer. DOS is a tool you use to manage the information your computer stores in disk files. DOS is a set of standard routines that your programs use to access the services of the components of your PC.

In the world of computers and computing, there is a gray area between the final programs that do something useful and the electronic and electro-mechanical components of the computer. DOS defines this gray area by providing computer users and their programs with a standard method for managing the computer's resources.

Companies that develop commercial programs rely on this standard method for gaining access to the computer's resources. Personal computer operators rely on this standard to be able to operate computers as word processors, database managers, electronic spreadsheets, and even diversionary game opponents. Because the core of DOS remains constant in its many versions, manufacturers of personal computer products as well as end users of personal computers have a stable operating basis for their work.

From your point of view, DOS is likely to be a set of commands typed on your keyboard. This is the practical, user's point of view. Learning these DOS commands takes you from seeing a personal computer as a mysterious box of complicated equipment to seeing a personal computer as the vehicle that affords you independence and productivity.

Introduction

MS-DOS QuickStart takes you through DOS step by step, describing the essentials you need to know about the operating system. The graphics convey overviews, relationships, and connections. The text supplies information that the graphics can't, provides comments on what you see, and explains abstract ideas.

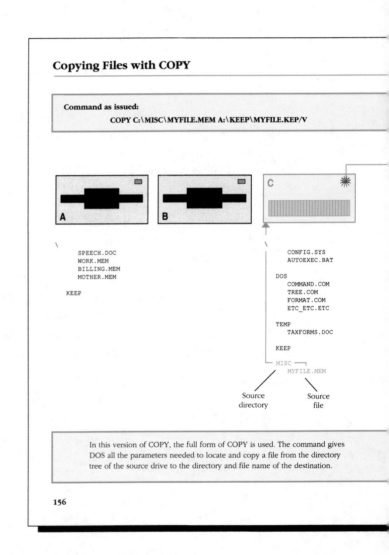

Copying Files with COPY

Command as issued:

COPY C:\MISC\MYFILE.MEM A:\KEEP\MYFILE.KEP/V

```
A                           B                           C

\                                                       \
    SPEECH.DOC                                              CONFIG.SYS
    WORK.MEM                                                AUTOEXEC.BAT
    BILLING.MEM
    MOTHER.MEM                                          DOS
                                                            COMMAND.COM
    KEEP                                                    TREE.COM
                                                            FORMAT.COM
                                                            ETC_ETC.ETC

                                                        TEMP
                                                            TAXFORMS.DOC

                                                        KEEP

                                                        └ MISC ┐
                                                            MYFILE.MEM

                                                        Source      Source
                                                        directory   file
```

In this version of COPY, the full form of COPY is used. The command gives DOS all the parameters needed to locate and copy a file from the directory tree of the source drive to the directory and file name of the destination.

Topics

Each chapter contains a group of topics, listed across the top of the right-hand page.

As you flip through the chapter, the highlighted rectangle moves from left to right, showing your location within the chapter.

In this example, the rectangle shows that you are in the topic called "Copying Files with Copy."

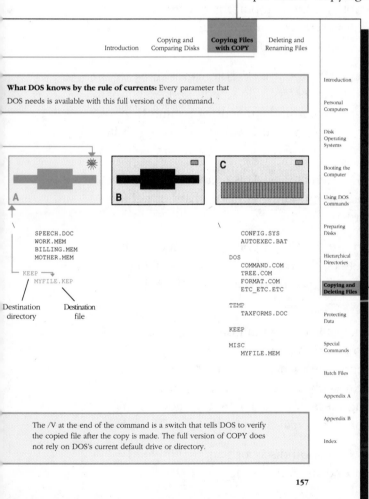

| Introduction | Copying and Comparing Disks | **Copying Files with COPY** | Deleting and Renaming Files |

What DOS knows by the rule of currents: Every parameter that DOS needs is available with this full version of the command.

```
\
    SPEECH.DOC
    WORK.MEM
    BILLING.MEM
    MOTHER.MEM

  KEEP
    MYFILE.KEP
```

Destination directory   Destination file

```
\
    CONFIG.SYS
    AUTOEXEC.BAT

DOS
    COMMAND.COM
    TREE.COM
    FORMAT.COM
    ETC_ETC.ETC

TEMP
    TAXFORMS.DOC

KEEP

MISC
    MYFILE.MEM
```

The /V at the end of the command is a switch that tells DOS to verify the copied file after the copy is made. The full version of COPY does not rely on DOS's current default drive or directory.

157

Introduction
Personal Computers
Disk Operating Systems
Booting the Computer
Using DOS Commands
Preparing Disks
Hierarchical Directories
Copying and Deleting Files
Protecting Data
Special Commands
Batch Files
Appendix A
Appendix B
Index

Chapters

Each spread lists all the chapter titles down the right margin.

As you flip through the book, the rectangle moves up and down, showing your chapter location.

In this example, the rectangle shows that you are in the chapter called "Copying and Deleting Files."

5

What Does This Book Contain?

Each chapter in *MS-DOS QuickStart* focuses on a particular DOS concept or operation. This book is specifically designed to get you to a comfortable proficiency in DOS.

Chapter 1 describes the components of personal computer systems: the display, the keyboard, the system unit, and peripherals. The last part of Chapter 1 traces the way computers handle data.

In Chapter 2 you learn the fundamental concepts of how an operating system works. Starting—or booting—the computer is covered in Chapter 3. The text and graphics show you how to start your computer with DOS V4.0 and with earlier versions of DOS.

Chapter 4 covers important concepts about DOS commands: how to use the command name, to add parameters, and to edit and execute a command. Once you have learned the fundamentals of issuing DOS commands, you are ready for Chapter 5, which covers preparing disks the computer can use.

Chapter 6 introduces hierarchical directories. This chapter clarifies the concept of hierarchy and explains the simple concept that lies behind DOS's method of hard disk organization.

Chapter 7 teaches you how to use the COPY command, which is the most frequently used—and may be the most frequently misunderstood—DOS command. You also learn to use the ERASE and RENAME commands.

Chapter 8, "Protecting Data," takes up the all-important topic of backing up your disk files. You learn how to safeguard your information by making backup copies. Chapter 9 introduces a number of DOS commands that are extremely useful, but that you may not need to use very often. Among these commands are the redirection commands and such "workhorse" commands as TYPE and CHKDSK.

Chapter 10 covers batch files. Here, you discover that creating and using batch files is a matter of obeying a few simple rules.

Appendix A summarizes the commands covered in *MS-DOS QuickStart*.

Appendix B covers DOS installation for both floppy disk and hard disk systems. Appendix C lists the most common error messages you are likely to encounter as you use DOS and offers suggestions for dealing with each error. Finally, a detailed index helps you quickly find the information you need on a specific topic.

Who Should Use This Book?

MS-DOS QuickStart is an easy guide for anyone just starting with DOS. Enough basic information is presented to help you get started quickly. And enough essential information is provided for you to refer to the book often as you gain experience. After you learn the fundamentals you may want to go on to learn more about DOS. Que Corporation publishes a full line of DOS books: *MS DOS User's Guide,* 3rd Ed., *MS-DOS Quick Reference*, and *DOS Tips, Tricks, and Traps.*

What Hardware Do You Need To Run MS-DOS?

The type of personal computer most likely to use MS-DOS is one that is compatible to a great extent with the International Business Machine Corporation's Personal Computer (IBM PC). COMPAQ®, Zenith® Data Systems, Tandy®, AT&T®, AST, EPSON®, Wang®, NEC, Toshiba, Sharp, Leading Edge®, Hewlett Packard, and many other companies manufacture or market MS-DOS based personal computers.

The computer should have at least 256 kilobytes (256K) of system random-access memory (RAM), at least one floppy disk drive, a display (screen), and a keyboard. These suggestions are minimal; most MS-DOS PCs sold today exceed these requirements.

For convenience and processing power, you may want to include a second floppy disk drive, a hard disk with at least 10 megabytes of storage capacity, a printer, and a color graphics display. You cannot use MS-DOS on most computers made by Apple Computer, Commodore®, or Atari®. These computers use operating systems that can sometimes be referred to as DOS, but their operating systems are not MS-DOS compatible.

1

Personal Computers

In this chapter, you will learn about

- The components of personal computer systems: displays, keyboards, the CPU, peripherals, and disk drives

- The concept of memory

- Disks and disk drives

- Computer systems and how they work with data

Until a few years ago, computers were large, expensive machines that were not available to individual users. But during the 1970s, advances in computer technology resulted in the production of smaller computer parts called chips. Most of the essential information a computer needed could be contained on one of these chips, or *microprocessors*. Computers that use these chips are called *microcomputers*. By the end of the 1970s, several companies had begun to sell microcomputers.

In the early 1980s, International Business Machines (IBM®) introduced the Personal Computer, which was an immediate success. Before long, the IBM PC captured the infant microcomputer industry and shaped its formative years.

Today, many manufacturers sell computers that are nearly functionally equivalent to the IBM Personal Computer. These computers have been dubbed *compatibles*. In this chapter you will learn about system elements that can be generalized to any IBM PC or compatible.

Key Terms Used in This Chapter

Display The screen or monitor.

Peripheral Any device aside from the main components that is connected to the computer to help it do tasks.

Disk A plastic or metal platter coated with magnetic material that is used to store files. A *disk drive* records and plays back information on disks.

Modem A device for exchanging data between computers through telephone lines.

Input Any data a computer reads.

Output Any data the computer puts out.

Bit A *binary digit*. The smallest discrete representation of a value a computer can manipulate.

Byte A collection of eight bits that a computer usually stores and manipulates as a unit.

K (kilobyte) 1024 bytes, used to show size or capacity in computer systems.

M (megabyte) 1000 kilobytes. Used to measure values or capacities greater than 999K.

Data A catch-all term meaning words, numbers, symbols, graphics, photos, sounds—any information stored in bytes in computer form.

File A named group of data in electronic form.

Components of Computer Systems

Personal computer systems based on the IBM PC are functionally the same, despite the wide variety of configurations available. As long as you have the main components, the shape and size of your computer matter very little. For example, you can find equally powerful machines in the traditional desktop configuration, in portable laptop models, or in compact lunchbox-sized computers. The wide variety of PC software operates equally well in any of these cosmetic configurations.

Hardware and *software* are the two main segments of a computer system. Both must be present for a computer to do useful work for its operator. They work together in a manner similar to a VCR and a taped movie. The VCR is like the hardware because it is electro-mechanical. The taped movie is like the software because it contains the information and control signals necessary for the VCR to display pictures on the TV screen.

Hardware is generally not flexible, whereas software is. Continuing the VCR analogy, you may, at one time, view a tape that contains cartoons. But the next viewing session, even though you use the same hardware (VCR), might be educational because the software (the video tape) stored different pictures and sounds.

Hardware

In general, the term *hardware* refers to the system unit, the keyboard, the screen display, the disk drives, and printers. Hardware includes all electronic and mechanical devices that make up or are used by a computer. The hardware of a computer system can be divided into *system hardware* and *peripheral hardware*. System hardware is directly associated with processing or computing activity. Technically, any device used by a computer for input or output of data is a *peripheral*. The subject of peripherals will be discussed later in this chapter.

Software

You can program (instruct) a computer to perform a wide variety of operations. Almost anything you can reduce to calculations can be made into a program and then entered into the computer. You probably use many small computers that have been programmed. Calculators, telephones with number memories, VCRs that can automatically record television programs, and arcade games are all examples of small computer-assisted devices that use a form of software.

You can teach your computer to perform chores much as these everyday appliances do. With the proper software, your computer will serve as a word processor, a spreadsheet, a project manager, a mailing list generator, or even a wily chess opponent! Table 1.1 illustrates some of the variety of software you can purchase for your computer.

Software provides instructions and information in electronic form so that the hardware understands and knows how to act. Software can be stored in various ways. The two most frequently used media are silicon chips and magnetic disks. Instructions on silicon chips is called *electronic memory* or just *"memory."* Disks provide *magnetic storage*.

The operating system is the most important type of software for the PC. Operating systems provide a foundation of services for other programs. These services provide a uniform means for programs to gain access to the full resources of the hardware. Operating systems that help programs to access disk resources are called disk operating systems.

This book is about the most common operating system for the IBM PC and compatibles. The IBM versions of DOS and the various versions of Microsoft® Corporation's DOS are highly compatible. For this reason, DOS will be used as the generic term to refer to both.

Components of Computer Systems

A computer system is a combination of certain hardware components. The components exist in a wide variety of configurations, but the computers all operate in essentially the same manner.

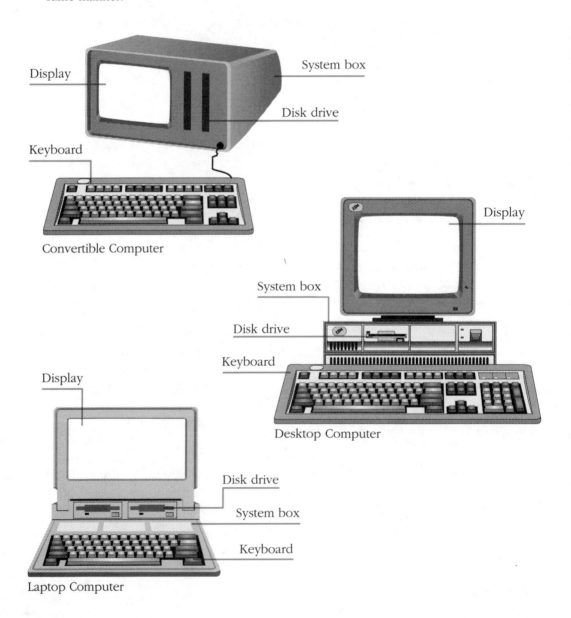

Display

System box

Disk drive

Keyboard

Convertible Computer

Display

System box

Disk drive

Keyboard

Desktop Computer

Display

Disk drive

System box

Keyboard

Laptop Computer

Table 1.1
Computer Software

Type of Software	Example
Operating systems	MS-DOS® (See Chapter 2); UNIX™
Databases	dBASE IV™; Reflex: The Analyst™
Spreadsheets	Lotus® 1-2-3; SuperCalc®; Quattro®
Word processors	WordPerfect®; WordStar®; XYWrite III™
Sales management	Act!
Utilities	SideKick®; DESKMATE (calendar, note pad, calculator)
Graphics	AutoCad; Map Master; Freelance®
Integrated programs	Smart©; Symphony®
Games	Flight Simulator
Home finance	Managing Your Money®
Desktop publishing	First Publisher™; Ventura Publisher®; PageMaker®

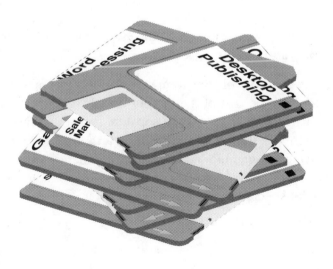

The Computer Display

The *display*, also called the *monitor* or the screen, is the part of the computer's hardware that produces visual output. The display is the normal or *default* location for output for the PC.

Most displays offered with PCs work on the same principle as your television set. Manufacturers also incorporate other types of technology into computer displays. For example, to produce flatter displays, manufacturers use a technology known as a gas plasma display. Gas plasma displays produce an orange color against a dark background.

Another technology adapted to computer displays is liquid crystal. Liquid crystal displays (LCDs) work on the same principle as digital watch displays. Most LCDs produce dark characters against a lighter background. The LCD works well in brightly lit rooms because the light striking the display increases the contrast of the display output. Some LCDs also employ a backlight that increases display contrast.

Regardless of the display type, all displays have one function in common. They take electrical signals and translate them into patterns of tiny dots or *pixels* that you can recognize as characters or figures. The more pixels available with a display, the sharper the visual image is.

The sharpness of the visual image, or the *resolution* is a function of both the display and the *display adapter.*

The display adapter controls the computer display. In some PCs the display circuitry can be part of the mother board (see "The System Unit and Peripherals"). It can also be on a separate board that fits into a slot in the computer. The display adapter can be a monochrome display adapter (MDA), color graphics adapter (CGA), enhanced graphics adapter (EGA), video graphics array adapter (VGA), or some less common type of special display adapter.

Text Display

When you see letters, numbers, or punctuation on your display, you recognize these images as text. This text comes from your computer's memory where it has been stored in accordance with the standard that most computers recognize, the American Standard Code for Information Interchange (*ASCII*).

Each ASCII code represents a letter or a symbol. These are sent to the display adapter so that you can see the characters on the screen. Because ASCII is the standard, the display adapter can use an electronic table to pull the correct pixel pattern for any letter, number, or punctuation symbol.

You may occasionally see references to extended ASCII codes. Here is what that term means. The ASCII-to-pixel table can have 256 different combinations, which is more than are necessary to represent all the letters, numbers, and punctuation in English. Display adapters use the leftover ASCII values for pixel patterns of lines, corners, and special images like musical notes.

In fact there are 128 leftover ASCII values for these special images. Programs can use combinations of these extended ASCII characters to produce boxes and other graphics-like characters. But if a program requires a pixel or some pattern of pixels on the screen that isn't included in the ASCII-to-pixel table, you are out of luck if you use a text type display. Of the various display adapters available, the monochrome display adapter (MDA) is the only adapter that is a text-only display adapter.

The Computer Display

Graphics Display

Graphics displays can produce any pixel or pattern of pixels. Thus, complex figures with curves and fine details can be displayed. The computer must work harder to create a graphics image than a text image, however. In order to light the correct point on the display, the display adapter must find the screen coordinate points for each pixel. No table of predetermined pixels exists as in text mode.

Graphics displays differ in the number of pixels available. The greater the number of pixels, the finer the detail of the display. Each pixel has characteristics that tell the graphics adapter what the color or intensity of the pixel should be. The greater the number of colors and intensities, the more storage space in memory is required. Graphics adapters offer varying combinations of pixel densities, colors, and intensities. Table 1.2 lists the various display types, showing the colors available and the pixel resolution.

Table 1.2
Resolution and Colors for Display Adapters

Adapter Type	Graphics Mode	Pixel Resolution	Colors Available
CGA	Medium resolution	320 × 200	4
CGA	High resolution	640 × 200	2
EGA	All CGA modes		
EGA	CGA high resolution	640 × 200	16
EGA	EGA high resolution	640 × 350	16
MGA	Monochrome graphics	720 × 348	2
MDA	Text ONLY	N/A	N/A
VGA	All CGA modes		
VGA	All EGA Modes		
VGA	Monochrome	640 × 480	2
VGA	VGA high resolution	640 × 480	16
VGA	VGA Medium resolution	320 × 200	256

The Computer Display

The image you see on a computer display is made up of pixels, a word coined from the phrase *picture element*. Using more pixels produces a sharper image. The sharpness of the image is called its *resolution*.

The higher-resolution image (left) of a girl's head uses four times as many pixels as the low-resolution image (above).

Introduction

Components
of Computer
Systems

**The
Computer
Display**

Keyboard
Variations

The System
Unit and
Peripherals

How Computers
Work with Data

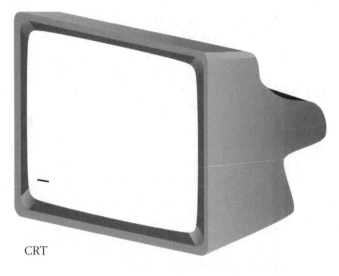

CRT

A blinking symbol on the
display (a box, an underscore
or some other character) shows
where the next character will
be placed on the display. This
symbol is the *cursor.*

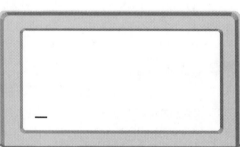

Gas plasma display

Liquid Crystal Display (LCD)

Keyboard Variations

Just like a typewriter, the keyboard of a computer contains all the letters of the alphabet. The numbers, symbols, and punctuation characters are virtually the same. The computer keyboard has the familiar QWERTY layout. (The name QWERTY comes from the letters found on the left side of the top row of letters on a standard typewriter.) But a computer keyboard is different from a typewriter keyboard in several important ways.

The most notable difference is the "extra" keys—the keys that do not appear on a typewriter. These keys are described in table 1.2. Depending on the type of computer you use, you will also find ten or twelve special *function keys*.

Many of the function keys are designed for use in combination with other keys. For example, pressing the Shift key and the PrtSc key in combination causes DOS to print the contents of the current screen. Pressing the Ctrl and PrtSc keys simultaneously causes DOS to continuously print what you type. Pressing Ctrl and PrtSc a second time turns off the printing.

The *function keys* are shortcuts. Not all programs use these keys, and some use only a few of them. When used, however, they automatically carry out repetitive operations for you. For example, the F1 key is often used for *online help*. Online help displays instructions from the computer's memory to help you understand a particular operation. The DOS V4.0 shell uses the F3 key to automatically back out of one operation and move into another. The F10 key moves the cursor to various parts of the screen. These and other keys will be explained in later parts of this book.

The keyboard is the way you put information into the computer. Each character you type is converted into code the computer can process. The keyboard is thus an *input* device.

AT Keyboards and Enhanced Keyboards

Many early PC-compatible computers use a standard keyboard like that of the IBM PC. Other machines use Personal Computer AT keyboards. IBM's new PS/2 computers use the 101-key Enhanced Keyboard. Some users prefer the keyboard arrangement of the standard keyboard, and others prefer the enhanced keyboard.

You can determine whether your computer has a standard keyboard, a Personal Computer AT-style keyboard, or an Enhanced Keyboard. Certain keys are found only on specific keyboards. For example, you find the Print Screen and Pause keys only on the Enhanced keyboard. You can, however, simulate these keys by using a combination of keys on the standard keyboard.

The 102-key Keyboard

Some new keyboards allow you to change key caps and switch key definitions for the Caps Lock, Ctrl, and Esc and ~ (tilde) keys. Northgate Computers, for example, not only offers these options, but also offers an enhanced keyboard. The enhanced keyboard locates the first ten functions keys to the left instead of across the top of the alphabet and number keys. The arrangement requires one more key than the 101-enhanced keyboards. Thus, the 102-key keyboard.

Non-standard Keyboards

Small computers, such as "lunchboxes" and laptops, use nonstandard keyboards, usually to conserve space. On some, space is so restricted that you need an external numeric keypad for use with software that performs advanced calculations.

Keyboard Variations

Table 1.3
Special Keys on the Computer Keyboard

Key	Function
Enter	Signals the computer to respond to the commands you type. Also functions as a carriage return in programs that simulate the operations of a typewriter.
Cursor keys	Change your location on the screen. Included are the arrow, PgUp, PgDn, Home and End keys.
Backspace	Moves the cursor backwards one space at a time, deleting any character in that space.
Del	Deletes, or erases, any character at the location of the cursor.
Ins	Inserts any character at the location of the cursor.
Shift	Enables you to capitalize letters when Shift is held down while the letter is typed. When pressed in combination with another key, can change the standard function of that key.
Caps Lock	When pressed to the lock position, all characters typed are uppercase, or capitalized. Caps Lock does not shift the keys, however. To release, press the key again.
Ctrl	The Control key. When pressed in combination with another key, changes the standard function of that key.

Special Keys on the Computer Keyboard (cont.)

	Key	Function
Alt	Alt	The Alternate key. When pressed in combination with another key, changes the standard function of that key.
Esc	Esc	In some situations, pressing it allows you to "escape" from a current operation to a previous one. Sometimes it has no effect on current operation.
Num Lock	Num Lock	Changes the numeric pad from cursor-movement to numeric-function mode.
PrtSc	PrtSc	Used with the Shift key to send the characters on the display to the printer.
Print Screen	Print Screen	Found on Enhanced keyboards. Same as Shift-PrtSc.
Scroll Lock	Scroll Lock	Locks the scrolling function to the cursor control keys. Instead of the cursor moving, the screen scrolls.
Pause	Pause	Suspends display output until another key is pressed. (Not provided with standard keyboards.)
Scroll Lock	Break	Stops a program in progress from running.
	Numeric Keypad	A cluster of keys to the right of the standard keypad keyboard. The keypad includes numbered keys from 0 to 9 as well as cursor-control keys and other special keys.

Keyboard Variations

<table>
<tr><td colspan="2" align="center">**Table 1.4**
DOS Key Combinations</td></tr>
<tr><td>*Keys*</td><td>*Function*</td></tr>
<tr><td>Ctrl-Num Lock</td><td>Freezes the display; pressing Ctrl-S or any other key restarts the display.</td></tr>
<tr><td>Shift-PrtSc
Print Screen</td><td>Prints the contents of the video display (print-screen feature).</td></tr>
<tr><td>Ctrl-PrtSc</td><td>Sends lines to both the screen and to the printer; giving this sequence a second time turns this function off.</td></tr>
<tr><td>Ctrl-C
Ctrl-Break</td><td>Stops execution of a program.</td></tr>
<tr><td>Ctrl-Alt-Del</td><td>Restarts MS-DOS (System reset)</td></tr>
</table>

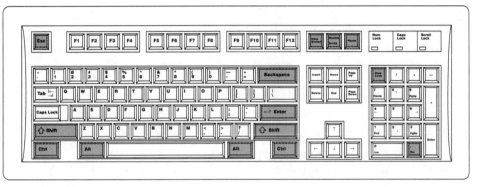

Extended keyboard

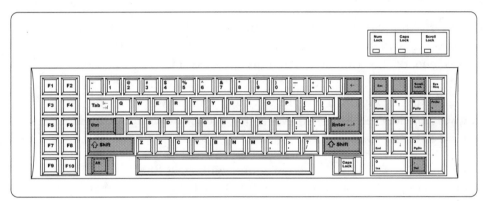

AT keyboard

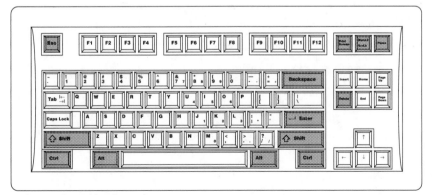

Space Saver keyboard

The System Unit and Peripherals

If you look at a standard desktop PC, you will find a box-shaped cabinet to which all other parts of the PC are connected. This box is called the *system unit*. The devices connected to it are *peripherals*. The system unit and the peripherals make the complete computer system.

The System Unit

The system unit houses all but a few parts of a PC. Included are various circuit boards, a power supply, and even a small speaker. System units vary in appearance, but a horizontal box shape is the most common. A vertical "tower" shape is becoming popular because it frees desk or table space.

The system unit houses the main circuit board of the computer. This circuit board, called the *mother board*, holds the main electronic components of the computer. The microprocessor and the various circuits and chips that support it are the primary components on the mother board. Normally there are electrical sockets where users can plug various adapter circuit boards. These electrical sockets are often referred to as *expansion slots*.

Chips that provide the computer with its memory are located on the mother board and, in some cases, an additional memory adapter can be plugged into an available expansion slot to increase the system's memory. The number of available expansion slots varies with the PC's manufacturer. Most mother boards have a socket for a math coprocessor. Math coprocessors help programs that are number-intensive do calculations more quickly and accurately.

Disk Drives and Disks

Disk drives are complex mechanisms, but they carry out a basically simple function. They rotate *disks*. Disks are circular platters or pieces of plastic that have magnetized surfaces. As the disk rotates, the drive converts electrical signals that represent data into magnetic fields on the disk. This process is called *writing* data to the disk. Disk drives also recover or *read* the magnetically stored data and present it to the computer as electrical signals.

When computers write to the disk, they store data as collections the operating system knows as *files*. Magnetically stored data is not lost when the computer's power is turned off.

You know that a drive is reading or writing to the disk when the small light on the front of the disk drive comes on. Generally, you should not open a disk drive door or eject a disk until the light goes out.

Two types of disks are available in a variety of sizes. Disks are either *floppy* or *hard*. Floppy disks are removable, flexible, and of lower-capacity than hard disks. Hard disks, also called *fixed* disks, are usually nonremovable, high-capacity rigid platters.

The components of a disk drive are similar to those of a phonograph. The disk, like a record, rotates. A positioner arm, like a tone arm, moves across the radius of the disk. A head, like a pickup cartridge, translates the encoded information to electrical signals. But, unlike phonographs, disk drives do not have spiral tracks on the disk's surface. The disk's surface is recorded in concentric rings or *tracks*. The tighter these tracks are packed on the disk, the greater the storage capacity of the disk.

Both sides of the disk are used for encoding information. Most MS-DOS computers operate in this manner and are thus called *double-sided* disk drives.

The System Unit and Peripherals

Floppy Disks

Floppy disks store from 360K to 1.44M bytes of data. They come in two common sizes. *Minifloppies* are 5 1/4-inch disks and *microfloppies* are 3 1/2-inch disks. The measurement refers to the size of the disk's jacket. Unless size is important, floppy disks are generally referred to as *floppies.*

Make sure that you know your drive's specification before you buy or interchange floppies. Floppies of the same size but with different capacities can be incompatible with a particular disk drive.

Fixed Disks

In 1973, IBM developed a hard disk technology and code-named it "Winchester." Over the years, the term Winchester has become practically synonymous with hard disks.

Hard disks often consist of multiple, rigid-disk platters. The platters spin at approximately 3,600 RPM, which is much faster than a floppy disk drive spins. As the platters spin within the drive, the head positioners make small, precise movements above the tracks of the disk. Because of this precision, hard disks can store enormous quantities of data—from 10M to more than 100M.

Despite their precision, hard disks are reasonably rugged devices. Factory sealing prevents contamination of the housing. With proper care, hard disks should give years of service.

Hard disks range from 3 1/2 to 8 inches in diameter. The most common size, 5 1/4-inches, holds between 2 1/2 and 10 megabytes of information per side.

Besides the display and the keyboard, a variety of peripherals is useful to a user. Many state-of-the-art computer programs require you to use a mouse to take best advantage of the program's features. Other peripherals, such as printers and modems, let you use the output of your computer as you want.

The Mouse

The mouse is a device that moves on the surface of your work space and causes the computer to correlate the movement to the display. The mouse is contoured so that your hand comfortably fits over it. The contoured shape and the cable tailing from the unit gives the vague appearance of a mouse sitting on the table. The mouse has one, two or three switch buttons that are positioned beneath the fingers of the operator's hand.

Not all software supports mouse input, but many popular programs do. Generally, mouse-based programs expect the user to point to options on the display and click one of the buttons on the mouse to carry out a task.

Printers

Printers accept signals (*input*) from the CPU and convert those signals to characters (*output*), which are usually imprinted on paper. You can classify printers in the following two ways:

- by the way they receive input from the computer, and
- by the manner in which they produce output.

The terms *parallel* and *serial* describe the two methods of output from personal computers to printers. And the terms *dot-matrix*, *daisywheel*, and *laser* are the generic names of printers that produce their output in three different ways.

The System Unit and Peripherals

Printers are usually rated by their printing speed and the quality of the finished print. Some printers print by using all the addressable points on the screen, much as a graphics display adapter does. Some printers offer color prints.

Parallel and Serial Printers

You connect printers to the system unit through a port. A *port* is an electrical doorway through which data can flow between the system unit and an outside peripheral. A port can have its own expansion adapter or can share an expansion adapter with other ports or circuits, such as a CGA.

The terms parallel and serial relate to the way the electrical data is delivered from the port to the printer. A serial port delivers the bits of the data byte one after another in a single-file manner. It takes longer to send one complete byte (character) using serial communications, but communications require fewer wires in the cable. Serial printers can communicate with the port over longer distances than parallel printers.

With a parallel port, all of the bits of data are synchronously sent through separate wires in the parallel cable one complete byte (character) at a time. Parallel printer connections are more common than serial connections.

Dot-Matrix, Daisywheel, and Laser Printers

All printers have the job of putting their output onto paper. Most of the time this output is text, but it may also be a graphics image. Three classifications of printers exist, distinguished by the mechanical method of getting output on the page.

The most common printer is the dot-matrix. Dot-matrix printers use a print head that contains a row of pins or wires to produce the characters. A motor moves the print head horizontally across the paper. As the print head moves, a vertical slice of each character forms as the printer's controlling circuits fire the proper pins or wires. The wires press corresponding small dots of the ribbon against the paper, leaving an inked dot impression. After several tiny horizontal steps, the print head leaves the dot image of a complete character. The process continues for each character on the line.

The daisywheel printer also steps the print head across the page, but strikes the page with a complete character for each step. All the characters of the alphabet are arranged at the ends of holders that resemble spokes on a wheel. The visual effect of this wheel is similar to a daisy's petals arranged around the flower head. Because the characters are fully formed, rather than made of dots, the quality of daisywheel printing is high.

Laser printers use a technology that closely resembles that of photocopying. Instead of a light-sensitive drum picking up the image of an original, the drum is painted with the light of a laser diode. The image from the drum transfers to the paper in a high dot density output. With high dot density, the output characters look fully formed. Laser printers can also produce graphic image output. The high quality text and graphics combination are very useful for desktop publishing.

Modems

Modems are peripherals that allow your PC to communicate over standard telephone services. Modems are serial communications peripherals. They send or receive characters or data one bit at a time. Modems can communicate with other modems at speeds from 30 to 960 bytes per second. Modems require communications software to coordinate their communications with other modems.

The System Unit and Peripherals

The arrangement of a hypothetical system unit showing
the placement of the hard and floppy disk drives and the
system board, also called the mother board.

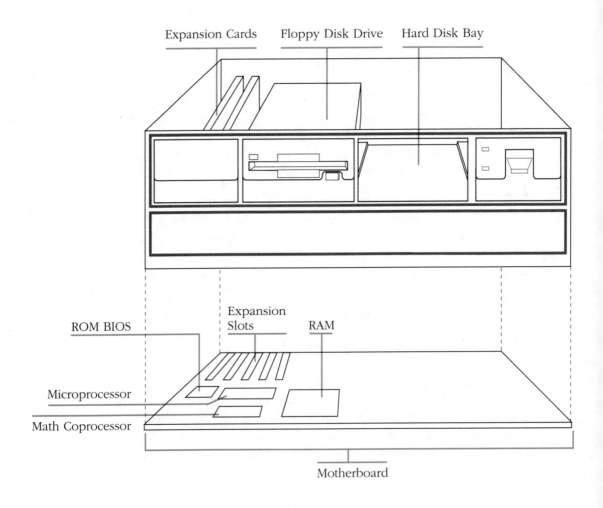

Expansion Cards   Floppy Disk Drive   Hard Disk Bay

ROM BIOS

Expansion
Slots   RAM

Microprocessor

Math Coprocessor

Motherboard

Hard disk platters are sealed inside the hard disk drive. Floppy disks are encased in either a flexible 5 1/4-inch jacket or a rigid 3 1/2-inch jacket.

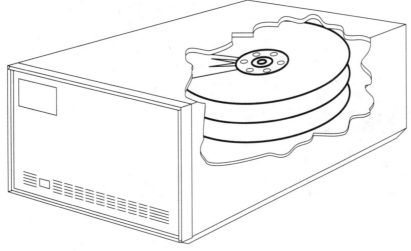

Hard disk drive

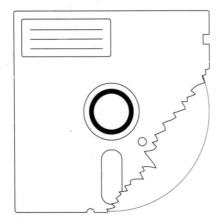

Floppy disk

Microfloppy disk

The System Unit and Peripherals

A mouse is a computer input device whose shape is vaguely reminiscent of a real mouse.

Joysticks are most popular for use in games and are used to enter information into the computer, as are keyboards.

A digitizer tablet provides a work surface that many users find more natural than using a mouse. The "puck" is moved across the tablet and the display shows the position of the puck on the tablet.

A modem allows you to transfer signals between computers by using telephone lines.

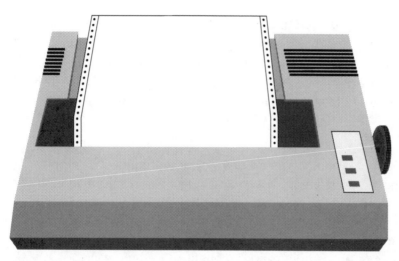

A printer is like a typewriter without a keyboard. It accepts input from the computer and renders it as characters on paper.

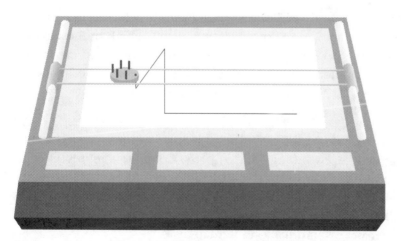

A plotter lets you draw with the computer. Unlike the printer, it moves up and down as well as back and forth.

How Computers Work with Data

Now that you have been introduced to the essential parts of computer systems, you are ready for a general overview of how these parts carry out the job of computing. The world inside a computer is a strange and different place. Fortunately, you do not have to know the details of a computer's operation to produce finished jobs. But if you do undertake some exploration, you will adjust more quickly to using your computer.

Computers perform many useful tasks by accepting data as input, processing it, and releasing it as output. Data is any information. It can be a set of numbers, a memo, an arrow key to move a game symbol, or just about anything else you can conceive. Input comes from you and is translated into electrical signals that move through a set of electronic controls. Output can be thought of in three ways:

- as characters the computer displays on the screen
- as signals the computer holds in its memory
- as signals stored magnetically on disk

Computers receive and send output in the form of electrical signals. These signals are stable in two states: on and off. Think of these states as you would the power in the wire from a light switch you can turn on and off. Computers contain millions of electronic switches that can be either on or off. All input and output follows this two-state principle.

The computer name for the two-state principle is *binary*, which means something made of two things or two parts. Computers represent data with two *binary* digits, or *bits*—0 and 1. For convenience, computers group eight bits together. This eight-bit grouping is called a *byte*. Bytes are sometimes packaged in two-, four-, or eight-byte packages when the computer moves information internally.

Computers move bits and bytes across electrical highways called *buses*. Normally, the computer contains three buses. The *control bus* manages the devices attached to the PC. The *data bus* is the highway for information transfer. The *address bus* routes signals so that data goes to the correct location within the computer. The microprocessor is connected to all three buses and supervises their activity.

Because the microprocessor can call upon the memory at any address and in any order, the memory is called *random access memory* or *RAM*. Some RAM information is permanent. This permanent memory is called *read only memory* or *ROM*. ROM is useful for holding unalterable instructions in the computer system.

The microprocessor depends on you to give it instructions in the form of a *program*. A program is a set of binary-coded instructions that produce a desired result. The microprocessor decodes the binary information and carries out the instruction from the program.

You could begin from scratch and type programs or data into the computer each time you turn on the power. But, of course, you wouldn't want to do that if you didn't have to. Luckily, the computer can store both instructions and start-up data, usually on a disk. Disks store data in binary form in *files*.

As far as the computer is concerned, a file is just a collection of bytes identified by a unique name. These bytes can be a memo, a word processing program, or some other program. The job of the file is to hold binary data or programs safely until the microprocessor calls for that data or program. When the call comes, the drive reads the file and writes the contents into RAM.

How Computers Work with Data

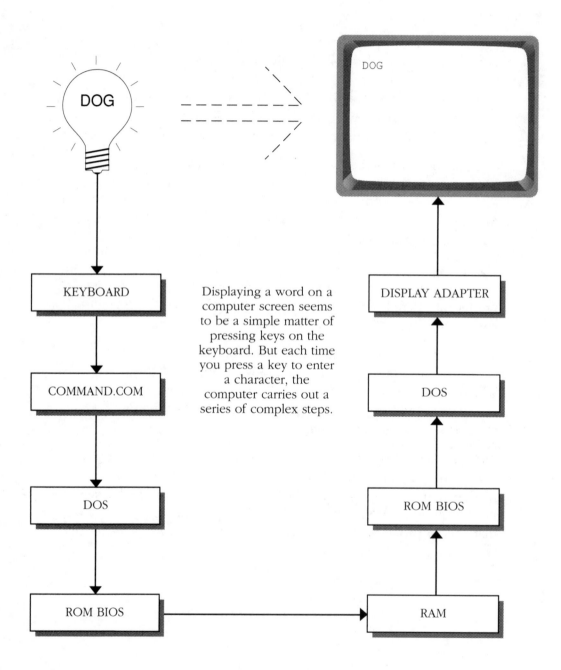

Displaying a word on a computer screen seems to be a simple matter of pressing keys on the keyboard. But each time you press a key to enter a character, the computer carries out a series of complex steps.

Address Bus

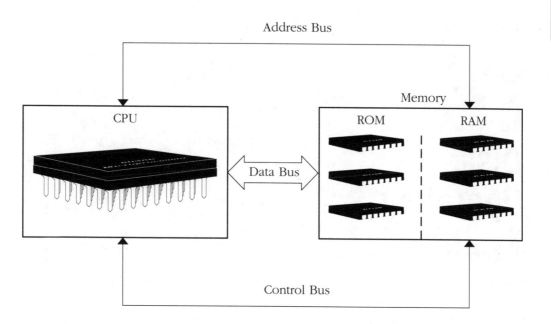

Memory

A personal computer is very busy on the inside. Program instructions held in random-access memory (RAM) are fetched and executed by the CPU. Resulting computations are stored in RAM. The CPU controls internal operations by using electrical highways called *buses*. The CPU uses the data bus to determine WHAT the data should be, the control bus to determine HOW the electrical operations should proceed, and the address bus to determine WHERE the data or instructions are located in RAM.

2

Disk Operating Systems

In this chapter, you will learn about

- The structure of DOS

- The uses of DOS

- The history of DOS

Chapter 1 introduced personal computer systems and their component parts, described software, and showed how data moves in the computer. This chapter introduces an important link between the hardware, the software, and you. This link is the *disk operating system* or *DOS*.

An operating system is a collection of computer programs that provide recurring services to other programs or to the user of a computer. If the computer's operating system did not provide these services, the user would have to deal directly with the details of the hardware. Without a disk operating system, for example, every computer program would have to contain instructions telling the hardware each step it should take to do its job. But because an operating system already contains instructions, any program can call on it. Disk operating systems get their name from the attention they give to the disks in the computer system.

IBM-compatible personal computers use MS-DOS, the disk operating system developed by Microsoft Corporation. Manufacturers of personal computers, such as Zenith, IBM, and COMPAQ, tailor MS-DOS for use on their computers. The manufacturers may put their own names on the disks and package different manuals with the DOS packages they provide. But all of these DOSes are very similar when they operate on a PC. When you read about DOS in this book, you can assume that what you read can be generalized to your manufacturer's version of DOS. In special cases, we'll point out differences.

Key Terms Used in This Chapter

Program   Instructions that tell a computer how to carry out tasks.

BIOS   *Basic Input/Output System.* The software that performs basic communications between the computer and the peripherals.

Redirection   A change in the source or destination that is normally used for input and output.

Applications program   A set of instructions that tell the computer to perform a specific task, such as word processing.

Interface   A connection between parts of the computer, especially between hardware devices; also the interaction between a user and an applications program.

Batch file   A series of DOS commands placed in a disk file. DOS executes batch-file commands one at a time.

Disk Operating Systems

Disk operating systems are collections of programs that carry out specific tasks. The kinds of files that hold these programs can be identified by the last three letters of the file name. These letters are called the *extension*. This list shows the names of the DOS files.

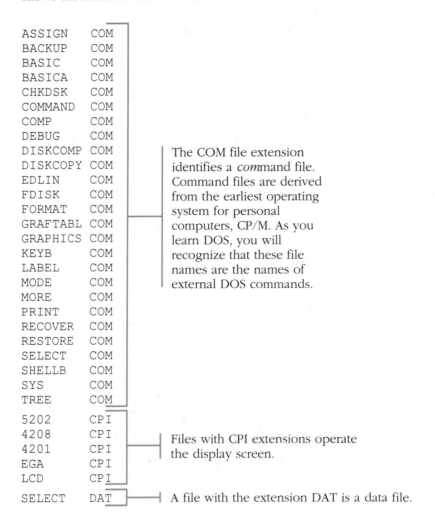

ASSIGN	COM
BACKUP	COM
BASIC	COM
BASICA	COM
CHKDSK	COM
COMMAND	COM
COMP	COM
DEBUG	COM
DISKCOMP	COM
DISKCOPY	COM
EDLIN	COM
FDISK	COM
FORMAT	COM
GRAFTABL	COM
GRAPHICS	COM
KEYB	COM
LABEL	COM
MODE	COM
MORE	COM
PRINT	COM
RECOVER	COM
RESTORE	COM
SELECT	COM
SHELLB	COM
SYS	COM
TREE	COM

The COM file extension identifies a *com*mand file. Command files are derived from the earliest operating system for personal computers, CP/M. As you learn DOS, you will recognize that these file names are the names of external DOS commands.

5202	CPI
4208	CPI
4201	CPI
EGA	CPI
LCD	CPI

Files with CPI extensions operate the display screen.

SELECT	DAT

A file with the extension DAT is a data file.

012345	678	Files used by a program that teaches aspects
012345	678	of DOS V4.0.
MORTGAGE	BAS	A program file written in the BASIC language.
AUTOEXEC	BAT	A batch file. In this case, a special batch file that runs automatically when you start the computer.
SHELL	CLR	A color configuration file that indicates to DOS V4.0 how to display the Shell program.
ATTRIB	EXE	
FASTOPEN	EXE	
FILESYS	EXE	
APPEND	EXE	
FIND	EXE	
IFSFUNC	EXE	
JOIN	EXE	EXE files are *executable* program files. Except for
MEM	EXE	technical details of their internal structure, they are
NLSFUNC	EXE	much like COM files.
REPLACE	EXE	
SELECT	EXE	
SHARE	EXE	
SHELLC	EXE	
SORT	EXE	
SUBST	EXE	
XCOPY	EXE	
SELECT	HLP	HLP files display on-screen assistance.
SHELL	HLP	
DOSUTIL	MEU	MEU extensions indicate that the files handle on-screen menus from which you make selections.
SHELL	MEU	
PCIBMDRV	MOS	These MOS file extensions identify files that
PCMSDRV	MOS	operate the mouse.
PCMSPDRV	MOS	
GRAPHICS	PRO	The GRAPHICS.PRO file contains profiles of graphics-mode printers supported by DOS V4.0.
ANSI	SYS	
CONFIG	SYS	
COUNTRY	SYS	
DISPLAY	SYS	
DRIVER	SYS	SYS files are *system* files. They are
KEYBOARD	SYS	also called *device drivers*.
PRINTER	SYS	
VDISK	SYS	
XMA2EMS	SYS	
XMAEM	SYS	

The Three Parts of DOS

DOS can be viewed as having three main functional components:

- the command interpreter
- the file and input/output system
- the utilities

All three of these components are contained in files that come with your DOS package. In the following sections you'll be introduced to the components and to their duties.

The Command Interpreter

The command interpreter is DOS's "friendly host." It interacts with you through the keyboard and screen when you operate your computer. The command interpreter is also known as the command processor and often is referred to simply as COMMAND.COM (command dot com).

COMMAND.COM prints DOS's requests on your display. When you enter a command, you are communicating with COMMAND.COM, which then interprets what you have typed and processes your input so DOS can take appropriate action. COMMAND.COM handles the technical details of such common tasks as displaying a list of the contents of a disk, copying files, and, of course, starting your programs.

The File and Input/Output System

The so-called "hidden" files are another part of the operating system. These two or three special files (the number depends on your computer) define the hardware to the software. When you start a computer, these DOS system files are loaded into RAM. Combined, the files provide a unified set of routines for controlling and directing the computer's operations. These files are known as the input/output system.

The hidden files interact with special read-only memory (ROM) on the mother board. The special ROM is called the ROM Basic Input Output System or simply *BIOS.* Responding to a program's request for service, the system files translate the request and pass it to the ROM BIOS. The BIOS provides a further translation of the request that links the request to the hardware.

In large part, it is the DOS input/output system, through the special BIOS, that determines the degree to which a non-IBM PC is "IBM compatible."

The Utility Files

The DOS utilities carry out useful housekeeping tasks, such as preparing disks, comparing files, finding the free space on a disk, and background printing. Some of the utilities provide statistics on disk size and available memory and compare disks and files. The utility programs are files that reside on disk and are loaded into memory by COMMAND.COM when you type their command names. They are often called *external* commands because they are not built into DOS.

By now, you no doubt suspect that DOS does many "technical" things that are not all that easy to understand. It is certainly true that much of DOS's activity falls into a category that could be called technical. But those DOS uses that you need to understand to make DOS work effectively for you are not at all difficult to understand. This section briefly described the common DOS functions you will use again and again as your computing expertise grows. Later sections treat each of these topics in detail.

The Three Parts of DOS

Disk operating systems insulate you and your programs from the need to know exactly how to make the hardware work.

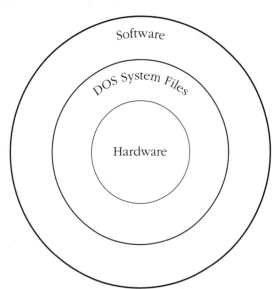

For example, to list the contents of a disk in a disk drive, you don't need to know the capacity or recording format of the disk or how to get the computer to direct the output to the screen. Another example: An applications program that needs to store data on the disk does not have to reserve space on the disk, keep track of where on the disk the data is stored, or know how the data was encoded. DOS takes care of all these tasks.

DOS provides a uniform service to the hardware by getting assistance from the permanent ROM BIOS in the computer. ROM BIOS can vary among computer makers, but the computers will be highly compatible if the design of the ROM BIOS is integrated with DOS.

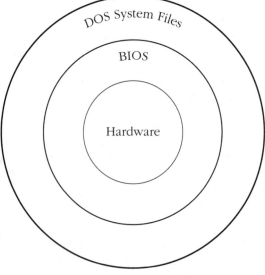

All of your communications with DOS are actually instructions to COMMAND.COM. COMMAND.COM is a special type of software that lets you address the file and input/output systems of the computer through the keyboard. Because you instruct COMMAND.COM, rather than the hardware directly, you need never know the details of how the hardware operates.

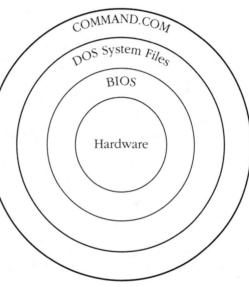

The DOS 4.0 Shell is a user-friendly program interface between your need for DOS services and the details of DOS commands. The Shell is a final layer that insulates you from having to know how to electronically control details of the computer's hardware.

What DOS Does

Managing Files

One of DOS's primary functions is to help you organize the files that you store on your disks. Organized files are a sign of good computer housekeeping. Good housekeeping becomes crucial once you begin to take advantage of the storage capacity available on today's disks.

Think, for example, about the fact that the smallest-capacity floppy disk can hold the equivalent of 100 letter-sized pages of information. Now, imagine that each sheet of information makes up one file: you have 100 files to keep track of. If you use disks that can hold more information than a standard floppy (such as a hard disk), file organization becomes even more crucial.

Fortunately, DOS gives you the tools to be a good computer housekeeper. DOS lists files for you, tells you their names and sizes, and gives you the dates when they were created. And you can use this information for many organizational purposes. In addition to organizing files, DOS can duplicate files, discard no longer useful files, and replace files with matching file names.

Managing Disks

Certain DOS functions are essential to all computer users. For example, all disks must be prepared before they can be used in your computer. This preparation is called *formatting* and includes checking disks for available space. Other functions in DOS's disk-management category are

- electronically labeling disks
- making restorable backup copies of files for security purposes
- restoring damaged files on disk
- copying disks
- viewing the contents of files on a disk

Redirecting Input and Output

DOS expects its input to come from a standard place, such as the keyboard. DOS sends its output to a standard place, such as the display screen. Designers of DOS recognized that it would sometimes be convenient to send output to another device, such as a printer. DOS designers provided DOS with the ability to *redirect*, or send in another direction, the output that normally goes to the standard output. Through redirection, a list of files that usually appears on the screen can be sent to the printer.

Running Applications Programs

Computers require complex and exact instructions—*programs*—to provide you useful output. Computing would be altogether impractical if you had to write a program each time you had a job to do. Happily, that is not the case. Programmers spend months doing the specialized work that allows a computer to function as many different things: a word processor, database manipulator, spreadsheet, or generator of graphics. Through a program, the computer's capabilities are applied to a task. Thus the term *applications programs.*

Applications programs are distributed on disks. DOS is the go-between that allows you access to these programs through the computer. By simply inserting a disk into a computer's disk drive and pressing a few keys on the keyboard, you can instantly have an astonishingly wide variety of easy-to-use applications at your disposal.

Applications constantly need to read data from disk files, to see what you have typed, and to send information to the screen or printer. These input and output tasks are common, repetitive computer tasks. DOS provides applications with an easy-to-use connection or program *interface* that sees to the details of these repetitive activities. As the user of the computer, you want easy-to-understand information about disk files, memory size, and computer configuration. DOS provides these services.

What DOS Does

Running Batch Files

Most of your interaction with DOS will take place through the keyboard. You type commands for COMMAND.COM to carry out. However, commands also can be placed in a disk file called a *batch file* and "played back" to COMMAND.COM. COMMAND.COM responds to these batches of commands from the file just as it would respond to commands typed from the keyboard. Batch files can automate often-used command sequences, making keyboard operation simpler. Difficult-to-remember command sequences are ideal candidates for batch-file treatment.

Handing Miscellaneous Tasks

Some of DOS's uses fall into a "miscellaneous" category. One example is the setting of the computer's clock and calendar so that files and applications programs can have access to dates and times. Or, you might need to use DOS's text editor to create text files like memos, notes, or batch files. You can even see the amount of RAM available for application programs through DOS.

The Importance of Knowing the Uses of DOS

By now, it should be clear that anyone intending to use a personal computer would benefit from some knowledge of DOS. Consider the fact that you can't use your computer at all unless you start it with DOS. Sure, someone is always more or less willing to do the DOS-related work for you so that you can avoid learning much about the operating system. But you will become much more proficient at computing if you learn a little DOS—and the computer results will greatly exceed the effort you spend learning DOS.

As you read the following chapters, you will find that DOS can be useful in a variety of ways. There are more than seventy DOS commands and functions possible. But this book emphasizes only those essential to using a personal computer for running off-the-shelf programs. You will quickly become familiar with the essentials of DOS through this easy step-by-step approach.

Here is a brief list of the important differences among versions of DOS, beginning in 1981.

Table 2.1
Quick Reference to Versions of DOS

MS-DOS Version	Significant Change
1.0	Original version of DOS.
1.25	Accommodates double-sided disks.
2.0	Includes multiple directories needed to organize hard disks.
3.0	Uses high-capacity floppy disks, the RAM disk, volume names, and the ATTRIB command. The ATTRIB command allows you to mark and unmark files making them "read-only." That means they can't be accidentally changed or erased while being used.
3.1	Includes networking.
3.2	Accommodates 3 1/2-inch drives.
3.3	Accommodates high-capacity 3 1/2-inch drives; includes new commands.
4.0	Introduces the DOS shell and the MEM command; accommodates larger files and disk capacities.

What DOS Does

Experts estimate that the typical personal computer user spends no more than 20% of his time actually using DOS. DOS facilitates the use of applications programs.

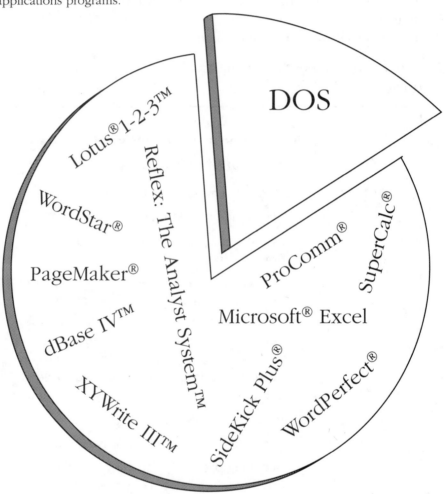

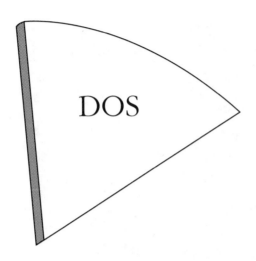

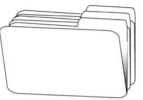

Helps you organize your
files on disk.

Redirects input and output.

Prepares disks and
safeguards their contents.

Executes the commands in
a batch file one at a time.

Handles miscellaneous tasks such as
setting the computer's internal clock.

53

3

Booting the Computer

In this chapter, you will learn about

- Cold booting DOS

- Setting the computer's internal clock

- Warm booting DOS

- Shutting down the computer

The first time you start your computer, you may not know what to expect. Once you learn a few computer terms and perform the basic start-up procedure, however, you will begin to feel at ease.

On early computers, operators started computers by entering a binary program and then instructing the computer to run the program. This binary program was called the "bootstrap loader" because the computer figuratively pulled itself up by the bootstraps to perform tasks. The term booting stuck. Today *booting* the computer still refers to the start-up procedure. Fortunately, the process of booting is simpler.

This chapter assumes that you do not know how to boot or know the process behind booting. A few commands are necessary to show you the start-up process, but don't worry if you do not know them. Just type in the examples and read in detail about the commands in later chapters.

Key Terms Used in This Chapter

Cold boot	The process of starting a PC from a power-off condition.
Warm boot	The process of restarting a PC while the power is on.
Cursor	The blinking line or solid block that marks where the next keyboard entry will appear.
Default	A condition or value that the computer, the program, or DOS assumes if you choose not to supply your own.
Prompt	A symbol, character, or group of characters that let you know you must enter information.
DOS prompt	The characters that COMMAND.COM displays to let you know that you can enter a DOS command. An example is C>.
Command	A text directive to COMMAND.COM, issued at the DOS prompt, that instructs DOS to provide a service.
Parameter	A directive used with a command that adds additional instructions.
Syntax	The proper formation of commands and parameters at the prompt so that COMMAND.COM can interpret them.
Logged drive	The current default disk drive that DOS uses to carry out commands that involve disk services. Unless you change the prompt with a command, the letter of the default drive will be the DOS prompt.

Booting DOS the First Time

The term *cold boot* assumes that the computer's power is off and that the unit is not yet warm. The word "boot" may seem odd to you, but it is the preferred expression. (Imagine telling someone that you have to cold boot your car!) Just remember that the key idea is that the computer's power switch is off. The next section reviews preliminary checks. Then you will learn how to do the cold boot.

Preliminary Checks

If you take airplane trips, you may have noticed that before taking off a pilot checks to make sure that all equipment is in working order. Just as this preliminary check of the airplane is important, so is your check of your computer's equipment. Preliminary checks help you avoid possible "crashes."

Computers like clean, steady power. Choose a good electrical outlet that does not serve devices like copy machines, hair dryers, or other electrical gadgets. Ask your computer dealer about a line conditioner if you must share an outlet. Make sure that the switch is off before you plug in your computer. Some computers have switches marked with 0 and 1. The switch marked 0 is the off switch.

Make sure that your PC has room to breathe. Computers must dissipate the heat generated by the electronic components. They do not need a blanket of paper to keep warm. Keep paper, books, beverages, and other clutter away from the system unit's case.

Place your DOS manual, DOS disks, and your PC system manual nearby for reference. The disk you use to boot your computer can be labeled "Startup," "System," "Main," or "DOS." Check your manual if you are not sure which disk is bootable or ask your computer specialist to provide a bootable DOS system disk. From this point on the bootable DOS disk will be called the DOS Master disk.

The Cold Boot

Insert the DOS Master disk in drive A. Check your PC's system manual for the location of drive A and for disk-insertion instructions. When you have properly inserted a disk, the label usually faces the top on horizontal drives and the left on vertical drives. If the disk does not go in, make sure that the drive doesn't contain another disk. Never jam or buckle a disk during insertion, because you could cause permanent damage.

After you load the disk, close the drive door. (Microfloppy drives close themselves.) If you have a lock on the front of the system unit, unlock the unit.

Finally, turn on the display switch, if necessary. Some displays are powered from the system unit and do not have a switch. Locate the computer's power switch. It is usually on the right side toward the rear of the system unit. Snap on the switch. At this point, the cold boot has begun.

If your computer supplier installed DOS on your hard disk, you can automatically boot from the hard disk simply by turning on the computer. To understand the elements of booting, however, you should learn to boot from a floppy disk.

Watching the Boot

The instant you snap on the switch, the computer's electronics do a Power On Reset (POR). The RAM, the microprocessor, and other electronics are zeroed out, which is something like cleaning the slate. The system then begins a power-on-self test (POST). POST ensures that your PC can deal with your valuable data responsibly. The POST can take from a few seconds to a couple of minutes. During POST you may see a description of the test or a blinking cursor on the display. When POST concludes, you will hear one beep and drive A will start activity. The bootstrap loader then loads DOS from the Master DOS disk into RAM.

Booting DOS the First Time

The cold boot consists of two steps: inserting the floppy disk in drive A and turning the computer's switch on.

You insert disks into horizontal and vertical drives in the same way. To complete the insertion of a 5 1/4-inch disk, close the drive door or turn the latch clockwise.

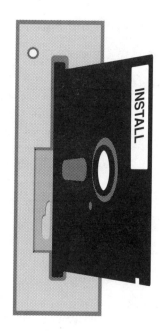

Insert 3 1/2-inch disks gently, pushing until you hear a click. The drive closes by itself.

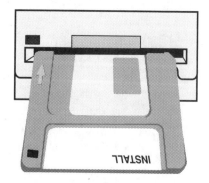

When you turn the power on, the computer performs a self-test to check whether it is working properly. Then the system prompt appears.

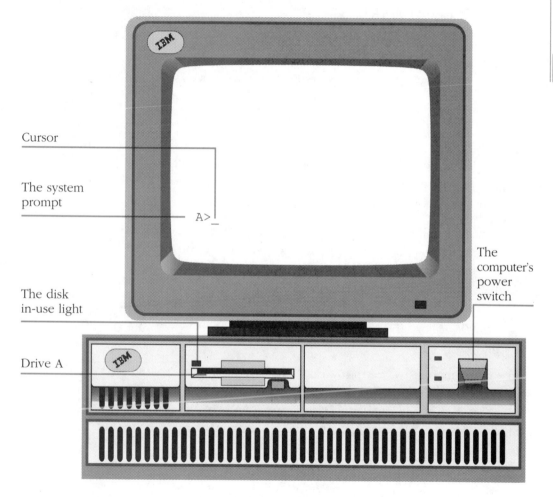

Cursor

The system prompt

A>_

Drive A

The disk in-use light

The computer's power switch

The Two Faces of DOS V4.0

With DOS V4.0, you have two view options:

- the prompt view
- the DOS Shell view

The *prompt* view is the traditional look of DOS. The prompt view appears on a plain screen with one letter of the alphabet representing the current, or active, drive. The letter is followed by a "greater than" symbol. The most common DOS prompts are A> for floppy disk systems and C> for hard disk drive systems.

The *Shell* view is the new look for DOS. The Shell view provides a full screen "window" with various menus, pop-up help screens, and graphic representation of directories and files. You may issue some standard DOS commands by pointing and selecting with a mouse.

The Shell view is the friendliest way to use DOS, but you should learn the basic commands from the prompt view. The reason becomes clear as you gain experience. With the Shell, you must learn not only the Shell commands, but the DOS commands for which they stand. And there is another complicating factor. It is unlikely that the Shell commands will be the same on the various compatible computers. The prompt view remains essentially the same.

Just remember that even though using the Shell is easy, you still need to know something about DOS commands and terminology. They remain substantially unchanged from previous versions of DOS. The Shell is simply a shortcut for someone who already understands the basics of DOS!

The First Look at the DOS Shell

If you have DOS 4.0, take some time to read this section. If you do not have DOS 4.0 installed, see Appendix A for installation instructions.

The Shell provides a visual presentation of DOS with "action options" from which you make selections. You can manage your computer from the action options, which are selectable versions of the DOS prompt-view commands.

This book presents the basics of DOS from DOS's command prompt view. But the Shell may be where your system starts after a boot. The following sections highlight the basic structure of the Shell.

The DOSSHELL Command

You type **DOSSHELL** at the DOS prompt to load the DOS Shell into memory if the Shell is not already loaded. DOS then establishes the system configuration selected when DOS 4.0 was installed. (A batch file holds the configuration commands for the DOS Shell.) For now, assume that the options selected are satisfactory for your computer.

The DOS Shell takes a few seconds to load after you enter the DOSSHELL command from the DOS prompt. If your system goes directly to the Shell, then it is not necessary to type the DOSSHELL command.

Start Programs is the first screen you see in the Shell. On either side of the screen title are the time and date. Under the title is the

The Two Faces of DOS V4.0

action bar, a line which displays the kinds of actions you can select. Positioned under the action bar are the group title line and the group contents. The Start Programs screen serves as your base to explore the important keystrokes you use in the DOS Shell.

On-line Help

Fortunately, you can always get information or explanations about DOS when you use the Shell. If you press F1, a help window appears. On-line help assists you with the current selection or action so that you can make an informed selection.

F11 displays a directory of different help topics. If your computer does not have F11, use the Alt-F1 key combination. You can press F9 to get a display of the keys and their Shell meanings. Within a window, you can move up or down a window's worth of text with PgUp or PgDn. The Shell sounds a beep when you press keys that it doesn't have an action for. Press Esc to cancel the help window and resume your session.

Moving from Shell To Prompt

You can move temporarily from the Shell to the DOS prompt, keeping the Shell in memory. To do so, use the cursor-arrow keys to place the highlighted bar on Command Prompt and press Enter. (The bar is called the *selection cursor*—a highlighted, reversed video, or different-color section of text that will be the object of an action if you press Enter or push the mouse button.)

When you press Enter, the DOS prompt appears. You now can enter DOS commands. To return to the Shell, type **Exit** and press Enter. For convenience, you can also press Shift-F9 to get to the command prompt. By selecting Command Prompt from the group items, however, you will see how the selection process works.

If you cannot move your selection cursor, check to make sure that Num Lock is off and that the actions on the action bar are highlighted or reversed in intensity. Use the right- and left-arrow keys to move the highlight accordingly. F10 moves the activity area of the selection cursor between actions and items. Press F10 until no action item stands out from the rest.

The other way to get to the DOS command prompt is to leave the Shell. This method causes the Shell to leave memory. To stop the Shell, press F10 and place the selection cursor on Exit. Now press ENTER. Move the selection cursor to Exit Shell and press return. The Shell returns you to the DOS prompt. Remember, you have exited the Shell, so you must restart the Shell by typing **DOSSHELL** when you want to use it again.

The Two Faces of DOS V4.0

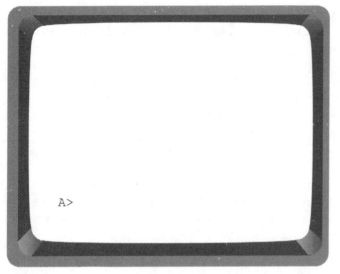

```
A>
```

The prompt view is the traditional, Spartan look of DOS: a plain screen with one letter of the alphabet representing the current, or active, drive and a "greater than" symbol. The most common DOS prompts are A> and C>, for floppy and hard drives respectively.

```
 12-19-88              Start Programs                3:08 pm
Program Group Exit                              | F1=Help
                        Main Group
            To select an item, use the up and down arrows.
        To start a program or display a new group, press Enter.

Command Prompt
File System
Change Colors
DOS Utilities...




  F10=Actions            Shift+F9=Command Prompt
```

DOS has a new look beginning with version 4.0. This version presents a new user interface, the DOS Shell. The Shell view is a full-screen "window" with menus and pop-up help screens.

Introduction

Personal
Computers

Disk
Operating
Systems

**Booting the
Computer**

Using DOS
Commands

Preparing
Disks

Hierarchical
Directories

Copying and
Deleting Files

Protecting
Data

Special
Commands

Batch Files

Appendix A

Appendix B

Appendix C

Index

1. Group contents   2. Action bar   3. Display title   4. Group title

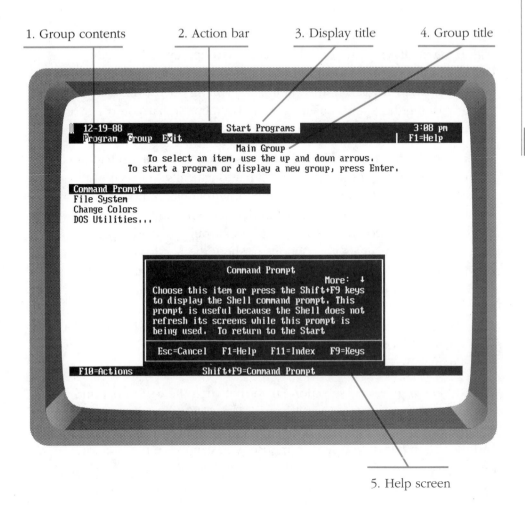

5. Help screen

The Start Programs screen is your beginning point in DOS V4.0. This screen lists the main items in the shell. You can add your own applications programs to this list to make accessing them easier.

DOS V4.0 also includes an on-line help feature. On this screen, the Command Prompt item is highlighted. Pressing F1 brings up information about the command prompt.

How To Navigate in the Shell

Now that you know how to get to the DOS command prompt from within the Shell, you can look at the Main Group items. The Main Group of the opening Start Programs screen shows the main areas where you will do work in the Shell. By selecting one of these items, you are asking the Shell to usher you to a screen so that you can work in that item's subject area.

When you select an action item and press Enter, additional selections pull down from under the selected item automatically. As with other selected items in the Shell, selected pull-down items are not carried out unless you press Enter. You move to other items in pull-down menus using the up- and down-arrow keys. You exit pull-downs by pressing Esc. The action bar gives you options for how the Shell presents the activity in the window below the action bar. In other words, you do DOS work in the lower part of the screen and give the Shell instructions with the action bar. The Shell knows the items in a selection list that aren't usable at that point and puts an asterisk in the item's name. If you have an EGA or VGA display, the Shell makes the item's name "fuzzy," rather than using the asterisk.

The F10 key toggles the selection cursor between the action bar and the lower work area of any Shell screen. Press F10 a few times and watch the selection cursor jump between the lower part of the screen and the action bar. If you have a mouse, you can move the pointer freely across area boundaries on the screen. One click selects an item. Two quick clicks select an item and tell the Shell to execute that item.

The Start Programs screen offers a Main Group of Shell items. These items come with DOS 4.0, but advanced users can add their own. Some software makers offer installation procedures for their programs that add their programs to the item list.

Use F10 to move the selection cursor to the Main Group's item list. Then try the arrow keys and watch the selection cursor highlight each item in succession.

File System Screen

The second item listed on the Start Programs screen is File System. Use the arrow keys to select File System and press Enter.

Since DOS is a disk operating system and since disks store information in files, the Shell pays ample attention to the file system in this screen. The general layout of this screen is like the layout of the Start Programs screen. You see an action bar toward the top of the screen. Notice that the action items aren't the same as on the Start Programs screen. Just below the action bar, the remainder of the screen is divided into sections that are bounded by bars or included in colored blocks. Look at the screen until you clearly see the individual sections. If you're familiar with DOS's hierarchical file structure, you'll see the screen's logic. Chapter 6 should clear up any confusion you may have about directories.

For now, you can concentrate on learning to move around this screen. Press the F10 key a few times. You see that the selection cursor toggles between the action bar and one of the lower items. F10 works the same here as in Start Programs. Press F10 until a lower item is selected. Press the Tab key. The selection cursor moves to an item in the next area of the lower part of the screen. Press the Tab key a few more times. The selection cursor moves from section to section. Use the Tab key to move to the next screen section. If you press Tab enough times, the Shell selects the action bar. You can tab so quickly that you may find using the Tab key more convenient for reaching the action bar than using F10.

How To Navigate in the Shell

Tab to the list of file names on the right side of the screen. Press the down-arrow key and see that the selection cursor moves to the next name. Use the up- and down-arrow keys to move to items that are listed vertically and use the right- and left-arrow keys on items that are listed horizontally. A beep tells you when you have reached the end of the list.

Press F10 again to move to the action bar. Press Enter to pull down additional information items about the selection. Use the left- and right-arrow keys to move to other main action bar items. You'll notice that the pulled-down list from the first selection allows the other item's pull-downs to appear automatically. You have all the selection possibilities available for viewing when you use the right- left-arrow keys. The File pull-down gives you actions for the Shell to perform on files and directories you have selected from the lower part of the screen. Options and Arrange pull-downs control the way the Shell shows the files and prompts you for confirmation when you erase or rename files.

Change Colors

If you have a graphics display adapter, select Change Colors from the Start Programs screen and press Enter. You are now in the Change Colors utility. The Shell allows you to pick from available color schemes to give the Shell the look you prefer. If you have a text-only display, the Shell knows that you can't change colors, so it won't let you try this item. If you have a black and white, green, or amber screen you'll see the colors as shades. Press the right- or left-arrow keys and your screen will take on a different look each time. Don't forget F1 for help if you need it. Look at all the combinations and stop on your favorite. Press enter to keep that combination and then press Esc to return to the Start Programs screen.

DOS Utilities Screen

The DOS Utilities screen is the last item on the Start Programs screen. All the selections in this group are disk utilities that allow you to set the date and time, copy and compare files, and format, back up, and restore disks. You'll learn how do do these activities from the DOS prompt in later chapters. For now, try setting the date and time.

Select DOS Utilities, using the arrow keys, and press Enter. You're now in the DOS utilities screen, but you're just passing through. Select Set Date and Time using the arrow keys and press Enter. A new block of the screen called a window pops up. This is a Shell pop-up window and in this case, it is the Set Date and Time utility.

You will see a prompt for a new date and a "picture" of what format the Shell expects. Press F1 for an explanation of the format. Then enter the date and at the cursor press Enter. Now you are prompted for the correct time. Enter the time at the cursor in 24-hour format and then press Enter. The Shell tells you to press any key, so press the space bar. The Shell brings you back to the DOS Utilities screen. From there you can press Esc to get back to Start Programs, F10 to move to the action bar, or Shift-F9 to get to the command prompt.

When you have finished entering the date and time, press Esc to return to the Start Programs screen. You have successfully navigated the DOS Shell!

How To Navigate in the Shell

[F1]   Displays a help window on screen.

[F10]   Moves the selection cursor between the action bar and the lower part of the screen.

[Tab⇄]   Moves the selection cursor from section to section on the screen. If you press Tab several times, the Shell selects the action bar.

[↑]
[←] [→]   Moves the selection cursor within a section of the screen or to select items in pull-down menus. In the
[↓]   File System area, use the up- and down-arrow keys to move to items that are listed vertically and use the right- and left-arrow keys on items that are listed horizontally.

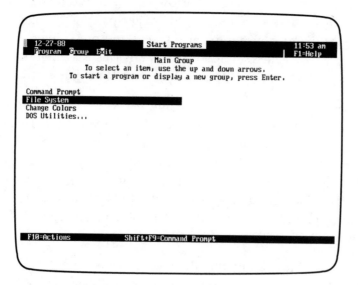

Use the cursor keys to move the selection cursor from item to item on the Start Programs screen. Press Enter to select an item. To return to the action bar, press F10. Shift-F9 moves you to the command prompt, but leaves the Shell in memory.

Introduction

Booting DOS
the First Time

The Two Faces
of DOS V4.0

How To Navigate
in the Shell

Completing
the Boot

The File System screen appears when you select File System
from Start Programs and press Enter.

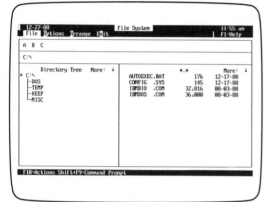

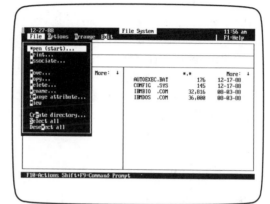

To change the logged disk drive, press
the left- and right-arrow keys. To move
between screen sections, press Tab.
Highlight items within sections by
pressing the cursor keys.

To display the file-system pulldown
menus, select an item from the action bar
with F10 and press Enter. Pressing the
left- and right-arrow keys displays menus
for other file-system options.

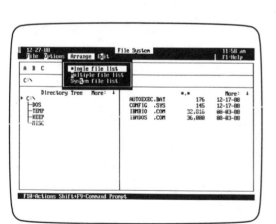

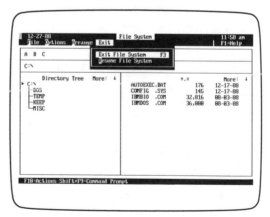

F10 or Tab returns you to the action bar from which you can select
another item or exit to Start Programs.

71

Completing the Boot

As you could see if you entered the date and time from the DOS Shell, the Shell itself can take you to the command line where you are prompted to enter information. For the purposes of the following discussion, assume that you are working from the command prompt, either because you do not use the DOS Shell or because you have used the Shell to reach the command prompt. The tasks covered here are miscellaneous items: learning to do a warm boot, setting the date and time directly from the command prompt, and learning about the logged disk drive. After reading this section, you'll be ready to take control of your computer with DOS.

The Warm Boot

The warm boot differs very little from the cold boot. For the cold boot, you inserted the DOS system disk and then switched on the computer. For the warm boot, your PC is already switched on. Make sure you have the DOS system disk in the A drive. You then press three keys.

Look at the keyboard, and locate the Ctrl, Alt, and Del keys. The warm boot takes no more effort than pressing, and holding, Ctrl and Alt and then pressing Del. The PC skips the preliminary tests and immediately loads DOS.

The DATE and TIME Commands

Most contemporary computers come with a built-in, battery powered calendar and clock. That means the correct date and time are the default values. A default value is a suggested response or recommended choice or action. If you make no specific choice when the computer prompts you, DOS accepts the built-in suggestion by default. You usually press Enter to accept the default.

You press Enter to activate the command you type. Enter is like a "Go" key that instructs DOS to execute a command. When a computer boots, it automatically enters the time and date from the system, offers default values, or requires you to enter each manually.

If your computer is set up to record automatically the date and time, you do nothing during the boot process. Otherwise, DOS prompts you to enter the correct date and time.

The Logged Drive

Once the boot is complete, the system prompt indicates the logged drive. The logged drive is the active drive—the drive that responds to commands. For example, an A> and a blinking cursor tells you DOS is logged onto drive A, which is usually a floppy disk drive. A C> and a blinking cursor means DOS is logged onto the C drive, which is usually a hard disk drive. You can change the logged drive from A to C by typing **C:** at the prompt and pressing Enter.

DOS remembers the logged drive as its current drive. Many commands use the current drive and other current information without your having to actually specify them in the command. You'll learn about this phenomenon later as the rule of currents.

Remember that you need not specify the drive if you are requesting information from the logged drive. (Note: If you are using two floppy drives, substitute B: for C: in the examples and exercises.) You'll learn later how to include the drive name when you request information from a non-current drive.

Completing the Boot

Memory check

```
ABC Computer Co.

Turbo

RAM check

640K

OK
```

Some computers let you watch the action of the power-on-self-test (POST).

Date prompt

```
Current date is Mon 01-16-1989

Enter new date (mm-dd-yy):
```

Unless you have an automatic system clock, you will need to enter the current date at the prompt.

Time prompt

```
Current time is 11:17:00.75a

Enter new time:
```

When prompted, enter the current time. You can include the seconds, but it isn't required.

System prompt

```
A>
```

You can enter DOS commands when the system prompt appears. The boot is complete.

Changing the logged disk drive

```
A>C:

C>_
```

Enter the drive letter
followed by a colon
and don't forget to
press the Enter key.
DOS reads the drive
letter and colon as the
disk drive's name.

Stopping the Computer

You may occasionally want to stop the computer from carrying out a command.
Besides switching the power off (the last resort), there are three ways to stop a
command in DOS:

Ctrl Break	Located next to the Reset key on some keyboards. Make sure you do not press the Reset key when you perform a Ctrl-Break. As in all Ctrl-key sequences, you hold down the Ctrl key and then press the other key(s) in the sequence. Ctrl-Break performs the equivalent of a cold boot on your system. For this reason, you may want to use Ctrl-C if you frequently type the wrong keys.
Ctrl C	Stops commands in which DOS pauses for you to type in further information. But be aware that DOS carries out many commands too quickly for you to intervene with Ctrl-C.
Ctrl Alt Del	The warm boot key sequence. Ctrl-Alt-Del should not be your first choice to stop a command, but sometimes Ctrl-C or Ctrl-Break will not work. If this approach fails, turning off the power is the last resort.

You can think of these key sequences as the "panic" buttons to stop DOS. Don't
worry that you will constantly have to use them to stop disasters. If you need to
use them, they will be handy.

4

Using DOS
Commands

In this chapter, you will learn about

- Issuing a DOS command

- Using the DIR command

- Wild-card characters

To communicate your need for service to DOS, you enter DOS *commands*. Commands are made up of groups of characters which are separated or *delimited* by certain other characters. A command you give to DOS is similar to a written instruction you might give to a work associate. Both the DOS command and the written instruction must communicate your intentions using proper form or *syntax*. Both must communicate what action you want carried out and what the objects of that action are.

For instance, if you need a sign on a bulletin board duplicated for posting on another bulletin board, you might tell a helper: "Copy sign A to sign B and verify that you have made no mistakes." Similarly, if you want DOS to copy the contents of disk A to disk B, you would give DOS the instruction: **DISKCOPY A: B:**. To verify that the copy is the same as the original, you would instruct DOS to compare the two disks: **DISKCOMP A: B:**. DISKCOPY and DISKCOMP are the DOS commands that say what action is to be carried out. A: and B: tell where the action is to be carried out. Although the instructions to duplicate a sign look more natural than the DOS DISKCOPY command, the two are quite similar.

DOS recognizes and responds to well over 50 commands. The most useful of these are built into the command processor and are immediately available at the system prompt. Because of this, they are called *internal* commands.

Other commands are stored as programs on your DOS disk or in a hard disk directory. Because these commands are loaded and executed when you enter them at the system prompt, they are called *external* commands. External commands can execute from the system prompt in functionally the same way as internal commands. Chapter 6 explains how.

Learning the "ins and outs" of issuing DOS commands takes some practice. Fortunately, there is a familiar structure to DOS commands, and you will soon branch out from examples to your own forms of the DOS commands.

Key Terms Used in This Chapter

Command   A group of characters that may be thought of as a word and that tells the computer what to do.

Syntax   The specific set of rules you follow when you issue commands.

Parameter   An additional instruction that defines specifically what you want the DOS command to do.

Switch   A part of the command syntax that turns on an optional function of a command.

Delimiter   A character that separates the "words" in a command. Common delimiters are the space and the slash.

Wild card   A character in a command that represents one or more other characters. In DOS the **?** represents any single character. The * represents the remaining characters in a "word" in the command.

Important Concepts about Commands

You issue commands to tell DOS that you need its operating-system services. DOS commands conform to standard rules in their command line entry. DOS is easier to use when you understand the concepts behind the commands. You can then generalize rules to different commands.

To begin to understand DOS commands, you need to know two fundamental facts:

- DOS requires that you use a specific set of rules or *syntax* when you issue commands.
- Parameters, which are a part of a command's syntax, can change the way a command is executed.

Syntax is the order in which you type the elements of the DOS command. Using proper syntax when you enter a DOS command is like using proper English when you speak. DOS must clearly understand what you are typing in order to carry out the command.

You can think of the command name as the action part of a DOS command. In addition to the name, many commands require or allow further directions. Any such additions are called *parameters*. Parameters tell DOS what to apply the action to or how to apply the action. Using DOS commands is really quite easy as long as you follow the rules of order and use the correct parameters.

Syntax

This chapter uses a symbolic form to describe command syntax. When you enter the command, you substitute real values for the symbolic name. Examples show you commands that you can enter exactly as shown.

DOS commands can have various forms that are correct. Even though the simple versions of DOS syntax work effectively, most DOS manuals show the complete syntax for a command, making the command look complex. For example, the syntax for the DIR command looks like this if we use symbolic names for the parameters:

DIR *d:filename.ext /W/P*

You use the DIR command to display a directory of the files stored on a disk. This command may look very formidable, but don't worry. Command syntax is much easier to understand if you look at the elements on the command line one at a time.

Some parts of a DOS command are mandatory—required information needed by MS-DOS. When you enter only the mandatory command elements, DOS in many cases uses default parameters. The command becomes very simple to issue.

Other command parts are optional. When you enter all syntax elements, DOS uses the exact instructions in place of default values. For the DIR command example, the **DIR** is mandatory. The rest of the command, *d:filename.ext /W/P*, is optional. Remember that d:filename.ext is a symbolic example of parameters. A real command would have actual parameters instead of symbols.

Important Concepts about Commands

You can type upper- or lowercase letters in commands. DOS reads both as uppercase letters. You must type the syntax samples shown in this book letter for letter, but you can ignore case. Items shown in lowercase letters are variables. You type in the appropriate information for the items shown in lowercase.

In the example, the lowercase *d:* identifies the disk drive the command will use for its action. Replace the *d:* with A:, B:, or C:. The *filename.ext* stands for the name of a file, including its extension. In DOS, file names can have up to eight letters. You can also have an extension, which consists of a period and up to three more letters. In this case you might type in the file name MYFILE.123.

Note that spaces separate or delimit the command name and some parameters. Other commands use the slash (/) character to separate parameters. Delimiters are important to DOS because they help DOS break the command apart. For example, DIR A: is correct; DIRA: is not. Try both examples, but use the letter of your disk drive. Typing DIRA: causes DOS to give you an error message. Bad command or file name is displayed when you do not use the proper syntax and parameters.

Switches

A *switch* is a parameter that turns on an optional function of a command. In the DIR example, /W and /P are switches. Note that each switch is a character preceded by a slash. Not all DOS commands have switches. In addition, switches may have different meanings for different commands.

You can use the /W switch with the DIR command to display a wide directory of files. Normally, the DIR command displays a directory with one file listing per line. The date and time you created the file displays next to the file name. As the screen fills, the first files scroll off the top of the display. The /W switch produces a directory that contains only file names and extensions.

Sometimes a disk may contain too many files to display on one screen. When you use the /P switch with the directory command, 23 lines of files, or approximately one screen, are displayed. The display pauses when the screen fills. At the bottom of a paused directory, DOS prompts you to `Press any key to continue` to move to the next screen full of files. The /P switch thus allows you to see all the files in the directory, one screen at a time.

When DOS says `Press any key to continue`, it really means to press *almost* any key. If you press the Shift, Alt, Caps Lock, Num Lock, or Scroll Lock keys, DOS ignores you. The easiest keys to press are the space bar and the Enter key.

Important Concepts about Commands

syn.tax \'sin-taks\ *n* 1: a connected or orderly system : harmonious arrangement of parts or elements

DOS is programmed to accept a limited number of instructions. These instructions must be issued in a specific form — that is, you must use the proper *syntax*. DOS's all-purpose response to an improperly formed command is `Bad command or file name`.

Syntax of the DIR command:

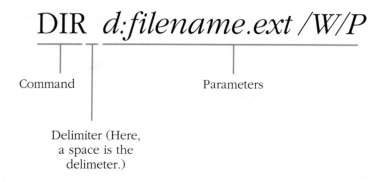

DIR *d:filename.ext /W/P*

Command

Parameters

Delimiter (Here, a space is the delimeter.)

DIR	An internal DOS command that lists the contents of a disk directory.
d:	A symbolic way of indicating a disk drive name.
filename.ext	A symbolic way of showing a file name and its extension.
/W	A switch that displays a directory in five columns.
/P	A switch that displays the directory 23 lines at a time.

To issue the DIR command:

1. Type **DIR**. Use upper- or lowercase letters. Press the space bar.

2. Type the disk drive name, if necessary—**A:**, **B:**, or **C:**.

3. Type the name of the file if you want to see the directory listing for a specific file.

4. Type **/W** for a *wide* directory.

5. Type **/P** for 23-line *pages* of a directory.

6. Press Enter.

Issuing Commands

Take a moment to become familiar with the instructions used for entering commands in this book. The notation helps you distinguish between what you type and what the computer displays.

Typing the Command Name

You enter a command when the screen displays the DOS prompt. This prompt usually consists of the drive letter followed by the > character. Notice that immediately following the > is the blinking cursor.

The command name is like a key to the DOS operating system. COMMAND.COM is the DOS command processor that reads the command you type. COMMAND.COM can carry out several "built-in" commands. It also knows how to load and run the external utility programs that you enter at the DOS prompt. Because you enter the built-in commands and the external commands at the DOS prompt, both are referred to as command names.

When you type a command, do not leave a space after the > of the DOS prompt. Enter all DOS command names directly after the prompt. If the command has no parameters or switches, then press the Enter key after the last letter of the command name. For example, you would type the directory command as C>**DIR** and then press Enter.

Adding Parameters

When you are to enter parameters that are not switches, this book will show them in one of two ways—lowercase and uppercase. You are to supply the value for the lowercase text. The lowercase letters are shorthand for the full names of the parts of a command. As in the command name, uppercase means that you enter letter-for-letter what you see.

Remember that you delimit parameters from the rest of the command. Most of the time the delimiter is a space, but other delimiters such as ., \, and : exist. Just look at the examples in this book to see the correct delimiter.

Introduction

Important Concepts
about Commands

**Issuing
Commands**

Using DIR To
Look at Files

If the example text has switches, you will recognize them by the preceding slash (/). Always enter the switch letter as shown. Do not forget to type the slash.

Ignoring a Command Line (Esc)

You will most likely make a mistake at some time when you are entering a command. Until you press the Enter key, DOS does not act upon the command. You can correct a mistake by using the arrow keys or backspace key to reposition the cursor. Press the Esc key if you want to type in an entirely new command. The Esc key withdraws the entry and gives you a new line. Just remember that these line-editing and canceling tips only work before you press the Enter key. Some commands can be successfully stopped with the Ctrl-C or Ctrl-Break sequence, however.

Executing a Command

The Enter key is the action key for DOS commands. Make it a habit to stop and read what you typed before you press the Enter key. After you press Enter, the computer gets busy and carries out your command. During the processing of the command, DOS does not display your keystrokes. DOS does remember your keystrokes, however. So be aware that the characters you typed could end up in your next command.

DOS Editing Keys

When you type a command line and press the Enter key, DOS copies the line into an input *buffer*, which is a storage area for commands. You can pull the last command line from the buffer and use it again. You will find this feature helpful when you want to issue a command that is similar to the preceding command you used. Table 4.1 lists the keys you use to edit the input buffer.

Issuing Commands

Typing the command:

```
A>DIR
```

Type the name of the command. Do
not leave a space between the >
symbol and the command name.

Adding a filename parameter:

```
A>DIR C:MYFILE.TXT
```

In symbolic notation, MYFILE.TXT
would be shown as *filename.ext*.

Adding a switch parameter:

```
A>DIR/W
```

The / is the delimiter. It tells DOS that a
switch is about to follow.

Ignoring a command line:

```
A>DIR C:MYF-
A>DIR C:MYFILE\
A>
```

To reposition the cursor, use the arrow
keys or the Backspace key. To restore the
system prompt, press Esc.

As you type command lines, DOS copies the characters into an input buffer. Use the keys in this table to edit the lines in the buffer.

Table 4.1
DOS Command Line Editing Keys

Key	Action
⬅ ➡	Moves cursor to the next tab stop.
Esc	Cancels the current line and does not change the buffer.
Ins	Enables you to insert characters in the line.
Del	Deletes a character from the line.
F1 or ➡	Copies one character from the preceding command line.
F2	Copies all characters from the preceding command line up to the next character you type.
F3	Copies all remaining characters from the preceding command line.
F4	Deletes all characters from the preceding command line up to, but not including, the next character typed (opposite of F2).
F5	Moves the current line into the buffer, but does not allow MS-DOS to execute the line.
F6	Produces an end-of-file marker when you copy from the console to a disk file.

87

Using DIR To Look at Files

It is important to know what files are on your disks and when you created them. You can manually keep a list of files, but it can be quite a task. Why not let DOS take care of this job for you? You can use the DOS DIR command to get a list of files that each of your floppy disks or hard disk contains.

The DIR Command

DIR stands for *DIR*ectory. A directory is a list of files. With the DIR command, you get a volume label, five columns of information about the files, and the amount of unused space on the disk.

Try the DIR command now. Type

DIR

and press Enter so that DOS can execute the command. You have just told DOS to display a list of files from the logged drive. You can also type **DIR A:** to specify drive A or **DIR C:** to list the files on drive C. The A or C is the optional drive parameter. If you specify no drive, DOS uses the logged drive by default.

You can change the logged drive by typing in the drive letter, a colon, and pressing Enter. For example, typing **A:** at the DOS prompt changes the logged drive to the A drive. A disk must be in a drive before DOS can make it the logged drive. Remember that you can only log to a drive that your system contains. By changing the logged drive, you can switch between a hard disk and a floppy disk.

Scroll Control

Scrolling describes how a screen fills with information. As the screen fills, information scrolls off the top of the display. To stop a scrolling screen, you press the key combination Ctrl-S. Press any key to restart the scrolling. On extended keyboards, press the Pause key to stop scrolling.

The Directory Listing

The first line you see in the directory listing is the *volume label.* A volume label is an identification that you specify when you prepare the disk. The volume label is optional, but can ease your organization of disks.

The next lines in the directory listing contain file information. Each line in the directory describes one file. You see the file name, extension, and size of file in bytes. You also see the date and time you created or last changed the file (assuming you entered the time and date when you booted your computer). Let's look at what this information means.

Filenames and Extensions

As you know, the file name contains two parts—the name and the extension. A period delimits the file name and its extension. In the directory listing, however, a space separates the file name from the extension.

In any single directory, each file must have a unique full name. DOS treats the file name and the extension as two separate parts. The file names MYFILE.123 and MYFILE.ABC are unique because each file has a different extension. The file names MYFILE.123 and YOURFILE.123 are also unique. Many DOS commands make use of the two parts of the file name separately. For this reason it is a good idea to give each file a file name and extension.

File names should help you identify the contents of a file. Because a file name can contain only eight alphanumeric characters and the extension three, meeting the demand of uniqueness and meaningfulness can require some ingenuity.

DOS is particular about which characters you use in a file name or an extension. To be on the safe side, use only letters of the alphabet and numbers, not spaces or a period. DOS truncates excess characters in a file name.

89

Using DIR To Look at Files

File Size and the Date/Time Stamp

In the directory listing, the third column shows the size of the file in bytes. This measurement is only an approximation of the size of your file. Your file can actually contain somewhat fewer number of bytes than shown. Because computers reserve blocks of data storage for files, files with slightly different data amounts may have identical file-size listings. This explains why your word processing memo with only five words can occupy 2K of file space.

The last two columns in the directory listing display a date and a time. These entries represent when you created the file or, in the case of an established file, when you altered the file. Your computer's internal date and time are the basis for the date and time "stamp" in the directory. As you create more files, the date and time stamp become invaluable tools in determining which version of a file is the most recent.

The last line of the directory tells you the total number of files that a disk contains and the amount of free space available. Free space is measured in bytes. This is useful when you want to determine how many more files a disk can hold.

Using Wild-Card Characters

Just about everyone has seen Western movies where a poker-playing cowboy says, "Deuces are wild!" Of course, this means that the number two cards can take on a meaning other than their own. Computer linguistics borrowed this wild-card concept and applied it to file-name operations on computers. You can use wild-card characters in file names to copy, rename, delete, list, or otherwise manipulate file names.

DOS recognizes two wild-card characters. You can place the ? character in any full file name. The **?** matches any one character in that position. The * in a file name or in an extension matches all characters in that part of the full file name.

Wild Cards in the DIR Command

You can use wild cards in conjunction with the DIR command. The following text provides examples in the use of wild-card characters.

The long form of the DIR command looks like

DIR d:filename.ext

Remember to substitute your actual drive letter for the **d:**. In place of filename.ext, type something like **MYFILE.123**. The DIR command you just typed tells DOS to list a directory of all files matching MYFILE.123. The directory listing would list only one file, MYFILE.123. When you use DIR alone, DOS lists all files in the directory. When you use DIR with a file name and extension parameter, DOS lists only files that match that parameter.

What if you want to see a listing of all files that have an extension of 123? You can type the command

DIR *.123

and DOS would list any file that had the 123 extension. For example, the files MYFILE.123 and YOURFILE.123 would display. If you issued the command **DIR MYFILE.***, you might get a listing of MYFILE.123 and MYFILE.XYZ.

You can name your letter files with a LET extension and your memo files with an extension of MEM. This lets you use the DIR command with a wild card to get separate listing of the two types of files.

The ? wild card differs from the * wild card. Only the character that is in the same position as the ? is a match. If you issued the command **DIR MYFILE?.123**, files like MYFILE1.123, MYFILE2.123 would appear, but MYFILE.123 would not. The same rules apply to other commands that allow wild cards.

Using DIR To Look at Files

```
Volume in drive A has no label
Volume Serial Number is OFDA-3762
Directory of  A:\

COMMAND   COM     37637 06-17-88   12:00p
ANSI      SYS      9148 06-17-88   12:00p
APPEND    EXE     11170 06-17-88   12:00p
COUNTRY   SYS     12838 06-17-88   12:00p
DISPLAY   SYS     15741 06-17-88   12:00p
DRIVER    SYS      5274 06-17-88   12:00p
CONFIG    SYS        99 10-14-88    8:23a
GRAFTABL  COM     10271 06-17-88   12:00p
GRAPHICS  COM     16733 06-17-88   12:00p
GRAPHICS  PRO      9413 06-17-88   12:00p
KEYB      COM     14759 06-17-88   12:00p
KEYBOARD  SYS     23360 06-17-88   12:00p
MODE      COM     23040 06-17-88   12:00p
```

```
NLSFUNC   EXE      6910 06-17-88   12:00p
PRINTER   SYS     18946 06-17-88   12:00p
VDISK     SYS      6376 06-17-88   12:00p
4201      CPI      6404 06-17-88   12:00p
4208      CPI       641 06-17-88   12:00p
5202      CPI       402 06-17-88   12:00p
        19 File(s)       57856 bytes free
```

Typing DIR at the DOS prompt produces a directory of the disk that is on the logged drive, but the display may scroll off the screen.

To temporarily halt scrolling, press Ctrl-S. Press any key to continue. On enhanced keyboards, you can also press Pause.

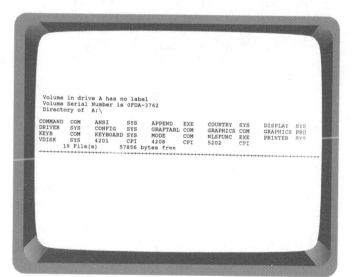

```
Volume in drive A has no label
Volume Serial Number is 0FDA-3762
Directory of  A:\

COMMAND   COM     37637 06-17-88   12:00p
ANSI      SYS      9148 06-17-88   12:00p
APPEND    EXE     11170 06-17-88   12:00p
COUNTRY   SYS     12838 06-17-88   12:00p
DISPLAY   SYS     15741 06-17-88   12:00p
DRIVER    SYS      5274 06-17-88   12:00p
CONFIG    SYS        99 10-14-88    8:23a
GRAFTABL  COM     10271 06-17-88   12:00p
GRAPHICS  COM     16733 06-17-88   12:00p
GRAPHICS  PRO      9413 06-17-88   12:00p
KEYB      COM     14759 06-17-88   12:00p
KEYBOARD  SYS     23360 06-17-88   12:00p
MODE      COM     23040 06-17-88   12:00p
NLSFUNC   EXE      6910 06-17-88   12:00p
PRINTER   SYS     18946 06-17-88   12:00p
```

The command DIR/P
displays the directory
listing page-by-page.

```
Volume in drive A has no label
Volume Serial Number is 0FDA-3762
Directory of  A:\

COMMAND  COM    ANSI      SYS    APPEND    EXE    COUNTRY  SYS    DISPLAY  SYS
DRIVER   SYS    CONFIG    SYS    GRAFTABL  COM    GRAPHICS COM    GRAPHICS PRO
KEYB     COM    KEYBOARD  SYS    MODE      COM    NLSFUNC  EXE    PRINTER  SYS
VDISK    SYS    4201      CPI    4208      CPI    5202     CPI
      19 File(s)     57856 bytes free
```

The command DIR/W
displays the directory
listing in a wide
arrangement, but you
lose information about
the individual files.

93

Using DIR To Look at Files

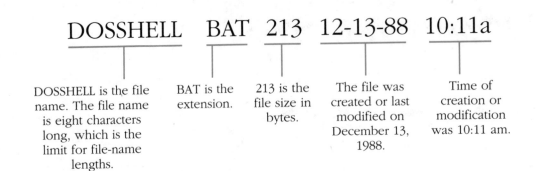

```
 Volume in drive A has no label
 Volume Serial Number is 0FD9-2E4E
 Directory of  A:\

 COMMAND   COM     37637 06-17-88   12:00p
 CHKDSK    COM     17771 06-17-88   12:00p
 DISKCOPY  COM     10428 06-17-88   12:00p
 PCIBMDRV  MOS       295 06-17-88   12:00p
 PCMSDRV   MOS       961 06-17-88   12:00p
 PCMSPDRV  MOS       801 06-17-88   12:00p
 PRINT     COM     14163 06-17-88   12:00p
 SHELL     CLR      4438 06-17-88   12:00p
 SHELL     HLP     66977 06-17-88   12:00p
 SHELL     MEU      4588 06-17-88   12:00p
 SHELLB    COM      3937 06-17-88   12:00p
 SHELLC    EXE    153975 06-17-88   12:00p
 DOSUTIL   MEU      6660 06-17-88   12:00p
 012345    678       109 06-17-88   12:00p
 DOSSHELL  BAT       184 10-14-88    8:22a
 SHELL     ASC         0 10-21-88    4:45p
        16 File(s)        35328 bytes free
```

The DIR command displays more than a list of file names. As your computing expertise grows, you will find many uses for the information provided by the full directory listing.

DOSSHELL BAT 213 12-13-88 10:11a

DOSSHELL is the file name. The file name is eight characters long, which is the limit for file-name lengths.

BAT is the extension.

213 is the file size in bytes.

The file was created or last modified on December 13, 1988.

Time of creation or modification was 10:11 am.

Wild Cards in the DIR Command

[?] With wild cards, you can tailor DOS commands. The ? replaces any single character in a file specification.

[*] The * replaces every character from the asterisk to the end of the part of the command where the asterisk is located.

[*] [.] [*] The wild-card filename replaces every character in the root file name and every character in the extension. *.* selects *all* files in a directory.

Examples:

DIR MYFILE.123   Presents directory information for the file MYFILE.123.

DIR *.123   Lists each file in the directory that has the extension 123.

DIR M*.*   Lists each file whose file name begins with the letter M.

DIR *.*   Lists all files in the directory.

DIR *.   Lists all files that have no extension.

DIR ???.BAT   Lists all three-letter file names that have a BAT extension.

DIR MYFILE.???   Lists all files named MYFILE that have three-letter extensions.

5

Preparing Disks

In this chapter you will learn about

- Preparing blank floppy disks

- Assigning volume labels

- Transferring the system files

- FORMAT's error messages

Before you prepare a floppy disk for use, it is just a round piece of Mylar in a plastic jacket. You must electronically adapt disks before you can store information on them. This electronic preparation process is called *formatting*.

DOS's FORMAT command performs the preparation process for disks. You do nothing more than enter the command. FORMAT analyzes a disk for defects, generates a root directory, sets up a storage table, and makes other technical modifications.

Think of unformatted and formatted disks as comparable to blank and lined sheets of paper. The lines on the sheet of paper provide you with an orderly way to record written information. The lines also act as a guide for the reader of your information. New disks (blank disks) are like blank sheets of paper to DOS.

When you format a blank disk, DOS *encodes*, or programs, data storage divisions on the disk surface. The divisions are concentric circles called *tracks*. DOS decides what type of drive you have and then positions the tracks accordingly. Each track is further divided into segments called *sectors*. DOS stores data in the sectors and uses the track number and sector number to retrieve the data.

A standard floppy disk (one that holds 360K of data) has 40 tracks per side. A standard microfloppy disk (720K) has 80 tracks per side. Disks with larger capacities have more tracks and more sectors.

Formatting disks will become a routine job for you, but remember to use care. Formatting erases *all* information that a disk contains. If you format a disk you previously used, everything stored on that disk will disappear. Be careful not to format a disk that contains files you want to keep. Labeling your disks helps you avoid such a mishap. Another precaution is to write-protect the 5 1/4-inch disk with a tab or set the write-protect switch on 3 1/2-inch disks. In any case, you should use the DIR command to see the files the disk holds before you attempt to format a previously used disk.

Format	Initial preparation of a disk for data storage.
Volume	A disk-level name that identifies a particular disk.
Track	A circular section of a disk's surface that holds data.
Sector	A section of a track that acts as the disk's smallest storage unit.
Internal command	A DOS command that is built into COMMAND.COM.
External command	A DOS command that must be located from a file and loaded by COMMAND.COM before it can execute.

Formatting a Floppy Disk

Blank unformatted disks are comparable to unlined paper. Formatted disks are comparable to lined paper. Just as the lines on the paper are guides for the reader, so are the tracks and sectors on the disk guides for the computer.

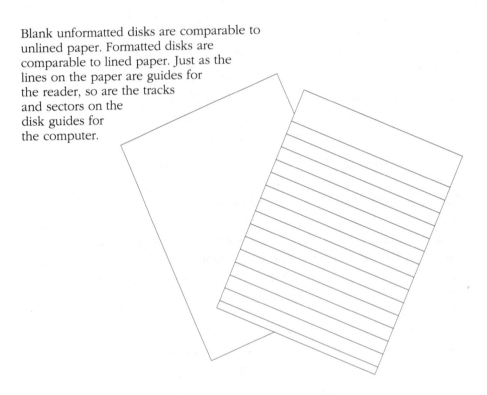

Anatomy of a minifloppy disk.

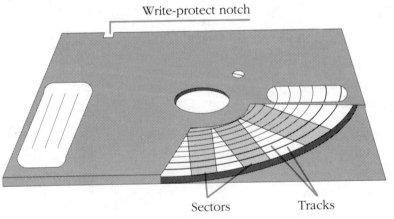

Write-protect notch

Sectors   Tracks

To format a floppy disk, write "Formatted" on the label and follow the directions for your system.

Floppy Disk Drive Systems

Insert the Working DOS disk into drive A and follow the directions for your system. (The DOS V4.0 installation process creates a Working disk. If you have an earlier version of DOS, you will need a working copy of the system disk. See Appendix B for instructions.)

```
A>FORMAT B:/V
```

```
A>FORMAT B:/V
```

Single Floppy Disk Drive System

1. Close the drive door if necessary.
2. Type the command and press Enter.

   Your computer treats your single floppy drive as both drive A and drive B.
3. Replace the Working DOS disk in drive A with the disk labeled "Formatted."
4. Press Enter.

Two Floppy Disk Drive System

1. Close the drive door if necessary.
2. Insert the disk labeled "Formatted" in drive B.
3. Type the command and press Enter.

```
C>FORMAT A:/V
```

Hard Disk Drive Systems

1. Check to see that drive C is your logged disk drive and that the C> prompt is displayed.

2. Insert the disk labeled "Formatted" in drive A.

3. Type the command and press Enter.

Formatting a Floppy Disk

```
A:FORMAT B:/V

Insert new diskette for drive A:
and press ENTER when ready...
```

The on-screen message tells you how to format a disk in drive B.

```
FORMATTING...

Insert new diskette for drive B:
and press ENTER when ready...
```

When you press Enter, the formatting process begins. The light on drive B glows.

Caution: Versions of DOS prior to 3.0 do not require that you specify the drive that holds the disk you want to format.

```
0 percent of disk formatted

.

.

.

Format complete

Volume label (11 characters, ENTER
for none)?_
```

DOS 4.0 indicates what percentage of the disk's surface is formatted. When formatting is complete, you may give the disk a volume name, using up to 11 characters, or you may press [↵Enter] to omit the volume name. The volume switch on DOS 4.0 is automatic.

```
362496 bytes total disk space

362496 bytes available on disk

1024 bytes in each allocation unit

354 allocation units available on disk
```

DOS displays a report for a formatted 360K floppy disk.

```
Format complete

   730112 bytes total disk space

   730112 bytes available on disk

FORMAT Another? (Y/N)
```

The displayed DOS report for a
formatted 720K microfloppy disk.

```
Format complete

   1213952 bytes total disk space

   115200 bytes in bad sectors

   1098752 bytes available on disk

FORMAT Another? (Y/N)
```

Ths displayed report for a formatted
1.2M minifloppy disk.

```
Format complete

   1457664 bytes total disk space

   1457664 bytes in bad sectors

FORMAT Another? (Y/N)
```

The next part of the report
prompts for additional
formatting activity. By
answering **Y**es to the
prompt and pressing Enter,
you can format another disk
while the format program is
loaded in system RAM.
Versions of DOS lower than
4.0 show the track and
sector numbers as
formatting proceeds.

FORMAT's Switches

As with many DOS commands, you can add switches to modify the
FORMAT command. You separate the switch from the command with
the slash (/) character. You can add more than one switch to a
command. For example, **FORMAT B:/V/S** is a valid command.

/V (Volume Label)

DOS reserves a few bytes of data space on disks so that you can place
an electronic identification, called a *volume label* on each disk. Think
of a volume label for a disk in the same context as the volume number
of a book. DOS 4.0 automatically builds this switch into the FORMAT
command.

After formatting a disk, DOS prompts you for an 11-character volume
name. You can use any of the following characters in any order:

- Letters A to Z and a to z
- Numerals 0 to 9
- Special characters and punctuation symbols:
  ~ ! @ # $ ^ & ( ) - _ { } '
- A space character (V3.3 and later)

When you enter too many characters or an illegal character in the
volume name, DOS 3.3 and later versions will use the characters you
typed, up to the mistake. Earlier DOS versions ask you for the volume
label again. If you do not want to name the disk, just press Enter.

/S (System)

The /S switch places the DOS system files on the formatted disk. Use this switch if you want to be able to boot your PC with the disk you are formatting. You cannot see these hidden files in the directory of the disk, but the files are there, along with COMMAND.COM, which you can see. The /S switch reduces the available storage capacity of the disk by about 80K.

/4

The /4 switch allows you to format a disk in a high-capacity disk drive for double-sided disk drive use. Use this switch to prepare a disk in your 1.2M drive for use in a 360K drive. Note: Despite this provision for downward compatibility, disks prepared in this way are often not readable on the 360K drive.

/1, /8, /B, /N, and /T

Primarily, these FORMAT switches allow current versions of DOS to format disks for very early computers or computers that use the first version of DOS. Although you may never need to use these switches, brief descriptions may be helpful.

/1 tells DOS to prepare a single-sided disk for use in a single-sided disk drive. /8 prepares a disk with 8 sectors per track. /B allows room for the system files on an 8 sectors-per-track disk. /N and /T allow you to vary the number of tracks and sectors on high-capacity disks.

FORMAT's Switches

Assigning a Volume Label

```
A> FORMAT B:/V
Insert new diskette for drive A:
and press ENTER when ready...


Format complete


Volume label (11 characters, ENTER
for none)?
```

You can place an electronic identification, called a *volume label*, on a disk. You must use the /V switch to assign a volume label if you use a version of DOS prior to DOS V4.0 Version 4.0 automatically includes the /V switch in the FORMAT command.

Legal Characters for Volume Labels

- Letters A to Z and a to z

- Numerals 0 to 9

- Special characters and punctuation symbols:
  ~ ! @ # $ ^ & ( ) - _ { } '

- A space character (V3.3 and later)

Formatting a Floppy Disk with System Files

```
FORMAT d:/S
```

This command allows you to format a disk with system files so that the disk is bootable. Remember to replace *d:* with the appropriate drive letter, A or B for floppy disk systems and A for hard disk systems, because you will normally use this command to format a floppy disk.

If you are using one floppy drive, your computer will act as though it has two drives. It will treat your single floppy drive as both drive A and drive B, just as in formatting without system files.

If you have two floppy drives, DOS will format the disk in drive B with system files. If you are using a hard disk, DOS will format the floppy disk in drive A.

When formatting is complete, a report similar to this one is displayed on your screen. This is a report for a 360K disk.

```
System transferred.

362496 bytes total disk space

108544 bytes used by system

253952 bytes available on disk

1024 bytes in each allocation unit

248 allocation units available on
disk
```

105

Understanding FORMAT and the Logged Drive

Earlier in the book, you learned that a single alphabetical letter, followed by a colon, designates a disk drive. When used in a command, DOS understands that letter and colon as the disk specifier. You also used the DIR command, which leaves the drive specifier out of the command line. In this case, DOS assumed you wanted a directory for the previously logged drive for its default.

The Concept of a Default Value

DOS uses certain prepackaged, or default, values to carry out its services. You can override many of these values through commands or switches. Some values, such as a /S switch for FORMAT, remain in effect only for one instance. Changing other defaults, like the logged drive, cause the default to change to the new value.

When you boot your computer, DOS automatically logs to the drive that holds the bootable disk. This drive is the default drive. DOS normally displays the default drive name in the DOS prompt, and uses this drive to execute commands. If the drive specifier is the same as the default drive, you do not have to enter the drive letter. If you want to issue a command to another disk drive, you must enter the drive specifier for that disk in the command line. The command is shorter and cleaner if you leave out the defaults. Many command examples you use in this book assume some default values. The logged drive is a frequently used default.

			Understanding	FORMAT's	Formatting a
	Formatting a	FORMAT's	**FORMAT and the**	Error	Hard Disk:
Introduction	Floppy Disk	Switches	**Logged Drive**	Messages	Cautions

Using FORMAT on Another Drive

COMMAND.COM contains built-in DOS commands, called internal commands. External DOS commands reside on disk. COMMAND.COM must find and load external commands before executing them. If the external commands are not on the logged disk, then you must enter a drive specifier *before* the command name. The drive specifier is the name of the drive that contains the command's program file. You will learn in the next chapter how to give DOS the correct path to the external commands.

Suppose that you want to format a disk in drive B. You have DOS loaded in drive A and a blank disk in drive B. Type **A:** and press Enter to make the drive holding the DOS working disk your default drive. Then type **FORMAT B:** to format the blank disk in drive B.

If you had changed to drive B, the FORMAT B: command would produce an error message. Because drive B is not the default drive, DOS would not find FORMAT.COM.

One solution to this dilemma is to issue the command **A:FORMAT B:**. DOS finds the format command on the DOS disk in drive A as specified in the command. The formatting is done on the blank disk in drive B as specified in the command.

The FORMAT command in DOS versions 3.0 and later requires that you specify the drive for the disk to be formatted even if the drive is the default. Prior DOS versions don't require you to name the drive in the command. Be careful not to format the wrong disk by default!

Understanding FORMAT and the Logged Drive

When you boot your computer, DOS displays the name of the drive that holds the DOS disk from which you booted.

This drive is the default (or current, or logged) drive.

To issue an external command to be executed from another disk drive, enter the drive letter for that disk drive before you type the command name. In this example, the FORMAT program is on the disk in drive A, and the disk to be formatted is in drive B. The logged drive is C.

Internal DOS Commands

BREAK	DATE	PROMPT
CHCP	VER	DIR
RENAME	VERIFY	COPY
DEL	RMDIR	VOL
CHDIR	ERASE	SET
CKS	MKDIR	TIME
CTTY	PATH	TYPE

COMMAND.COM must find and load external commands before it can execute the commands. Internal commands are built into DOS. You can issue internal commands regardless of which drive is the logged (current) drive.

Common External DOS Commands

BACKUP	DISKCOPY	RESTORE
CHDIR (CD)	ECHO	RMDIR (RD)
CHKDSK	ERASE	SORT
CLS	FIND	SYS
COPY	FORMAT	TIME
DATE	MKDIR (MD)	TREE
DELETE	MORE	TYPE
DEVICE	PATH	VER
DIR	PROMPT	VERIFY
DISKCOMP	RENAME	VOL

With external commands like FORMAT, DOS prompts you to place the proper disk into the drive before the command is carried out. If you have a floppy disk system, you can remove the DOS working copy that contains the FORMAT program, insert the disk to be formatted, and press any key.

109

FORMAT's Error Messages

Errors that can occur during formatting activity are usually not serious. For example, if you insert a blank disk in the drive where DOS expects to find the FORMAT command *before* you issue the FORMAT command, DOS displays the message:

```
General Failure Reading Drive A
Abort, Retry, Fail?
```

Since DOS could not find the internal file tables on the blank disk when it attempted to load FORMAT, DOS assumed that the disk, the drive, or the drive electronics had failed. The solution is to place the DOS disk in the drive and answer the prompt **R** to retry.

When you insert and remove disks during formatting sessions, you can give DOS the "go ahead" too soon when you are prompted to Press any key when ready. When you make this error, DOS displays the message:

```
Not Ready Error Reading in Drive A
Abort, Retry, Fail?
```

This message usually means that the drive door is still open or that you forgot to insert a disk into the drive. An open drive door isn't uncommon when you are swapping disks in and out of floppy disk drives. To recover, make sure the disk is properly inserted in the drive, close the drive door, and enter **R** at the prompt.

These first two error conditions happen during formatting activity, but they could happen as you use other DOS commands as well. These errors aren't FORMAT's errors, but since FORMAT is an external command and FORMAT works on blank disks, these errors are likely to occur with FORMAT.

If the FORMAT command detects errors on the disk, you will see a line describing the problem in the report. For example, the line might state

```
2048 bytes in bad sectors
```

The `bytes in bad sectors` message means that MS-DOS found bad sectors on the disk. These sectors cannot be used to hold information. The total amount of free space on the disk is reduced by the number of bytes in bad sectors.

You can have your dealer replace a floppy disk, or you can use the disk as is. Before you do either, though, try formatting the disk again. Some disks do not format properly the first time. If, after the second format attempt, the bad sector message is still present, you may want to use a different disk. Bad sectors can cause trouble with the disk.

You can usually run FORMAT a second time by answering Y to the question `Format another (Y/N)?` , and pressing Enter.

The worst disk error message is:

```
Invalid media or track 0 bad - disk unusable
```

This message may mean that the areas on the disk that hold key DOS system data are bad. If you get the `disk unusable` error message, take the disk back to your dealer if you just bought it. If the disk is old, throw it away.

The `invalid media` message may stem from your use of a disk whose capacity is wrong for your computer system. The magnetic oxides on disk surfaces differ among particular capacities. Using a higher capacity disk than necessary will cause disk errors.

Some systems are set up with a RAM disk. A RAM disk is a portion of system memory that software treats collectively as a disk drive. RAM disks are also called virtual disks or memory disks. You cannot format a RAM disk.

FORMAT's Error Messages

```
A>FORMAT A:/U

General failure reading drive A
Abort, Retry, Fail?
```

The disk is not correctly formatted, the disk's formatting is wrong for the computer you are using, or the disk is damaged.

Format the disk again, making sure that the disk is formatted for your system. If the disk is damaged, replace it.

```
C>FORMAT A:
Insert new diskette for drive A:
and press ENTER when ready...


Not ready
Format terminated
Format another (Y/N)?
```

DOS was unable to read from the disk drive. For floppy disk drives, the drive door may be open or the disk may not be inserted.

Remove the disk and reinsert it, close the drive door if necessary, and issue the FORMAT command again. Abort the operation by typing **A**.

```
A>FORMAT A:/U


A>FORMAT A:/U
Insert new diskette for drive A:
and press ENTER when ready...


Write protect error
Format terminated
Format another (Y/N)?
```

This error occurred because DOS attempted to format a write-protected disk. Write protection saved the disk from accidental erasure.

```
A>FORMAT A:
Insert new diskette for drive A:
and press ENTER when ready...

Invalid media or Track 0 bad - disk unusable
Format terminated
Format another (Y/N)?N
A>
```

This disk had a scratched surface, and DOS was unable to read disk-level information on the first track. This disk must be discarded.

```
C>FORMAT A:
Insert new diskette for drive A:
and press ENTER when ready...

Format complete

Volume label (11 characters, ENTER for none)?

    1213952 bytes total disk space
     107520 bytes in bad sectors
    1106432 bytes available on disk

        512 bytes in each allocation unit
       2161 allocation units available on disk

Volume Serial Number is 0B75-13FB

Format another (Y/N)?
```

Bad sectors cannot hold information on the disk. Thus, the total amount of free space is reduced by the number of bytes in bad sectors.

Try reformatting the disk. If it still has bad sectors, you can have your dealer replace the disk, or you can use the disk as is. Before you do either, though, try formatting the disk again.

```
A>FORMAT A:

General failure reading drive A
Abort, Retry, Fail?R

General failure reading drive A
Abort, Retry, Fail?f
Invalid drive specification
Insert new diskette for drive A:
and press ENTER when ready...
```

Some disks do not format properly the first time. If, after the second format attempt, the error message is still present, you may want to use a different disk. Bad sectors can cause trouble with the disk.

113

Formatting a Hard Disk: Cautions

Many computer dealers install the operating system on a computer's hard disk before you receive it. If your dealer has installed an applications program, such as a word processor, **do not format the hard disk**. If you re-format your hard disk, all programs and data will be erased.

Hard disks are a desirable part of a computer system because of their speed and storage capacity. And, just like floppy disks, they must be formatted before you use them. Unless you are very familiar with the procedure, however, **DO NOT ATTEMPT TO FORMAT YOUR HARD DISK!**

If you purchased your hard disk separately from your computer, consult the guide that came with your drive for installation instructions. The space in this book does not allow for a discussion of the many variations of hard-disk installation. If you bought the drive from a full-service dealer, ask for assistance.

Before you attempt to format your hard disk, do a complete back-up. Make sure that you are familiar with the RESTORE command (see Chapter 8). You also should have a bootable floppy disk with a copy of the RESTORE program on it. *The MS-DOS User's Guide,* 3rd Ed. devotes several pages to preparing and formatting a hard disk. If you *must* format your hard disk, consult that book or your computer's manual.

Remember that FORMAT erases all data that a disk contains. Always check the directory of the disk you want to format. It may contain data you need. Make a mental note to check the command line thoroughly when you use the FORMAT command. For example, if you are used to typing **C:** as a drive specifier, habit might send you into a disastrous format mistake.

It is a good policy to format your hard disk at least once a year. Why? Because accumulating and erasing files fragments individual files across the disk. Backing up the disk, formatting the disk, and restoring the backed up files "restores" the disk's speed performance. However, using a software program designed to improve your hard disk's performance is a better and safer alternative than formatting. Disk Optimizer™ is one such program, but other programs exist. Ask your computer hardware or software dealer which one might be best for your system.

6

Hierarchical
Directories

In this chapter, you will learn about

- Organizing disks with hierarchical directories

- Setting up subdirectories

- Moving through directories using path names

- Hierarchical directory commands and how to use them

In Chapter 4, you learned how to issue the DIR command to see a listing of the contents of a disk directory. A disk directory is not only a file list that you see on-screen, but also an internal software list. The directory is the disk's "letter of introduction" to your computer. In this chapter, you will learn more about important directory commands.

This chapter explains DOS's hierarchical directory structure. You will learn how to use the hierarchical structure to group and organize files. You also will learn how to use the PATH command to move around your hard disk in a logical way. This chapter introduces DOS commands that deal directly with directory organization.

Key Terms Used in This Chapter

Hierarchical directory	An organizational structure used by DOS to segregate files into levels of subdirectories.

Tree structure	A term applied to hierarchical directories to describe the conceptual scheme in which directories "belong" to higher directories and "own" lower directories. Viewed graphically, the ownership relationships resemble an inverted tree.
Directory	An area of the DOS file system that holds information about files and directories.
Root directory	The highest directory of the tree structure of DOS. All DOS disks have a root directory, which is automatically created by DOS (versions 2.0 and later).
Subdirectory	A directory created in another directory and subordinate to that directory. Also referred to simply as a directory.
Directory specifier	A DOS command parameter that tells DOS where to find a file or where to carry out a command.
Path name	Another name for the directory specifier. The path name gives DOS the directions it needs to trace the directory tree to the directory containing desired commands or files.
	The backslash. The character DOS expects to see in a command to separate directory names. By itself as a parameter, the backslash signifies the root directory.
PATH command	The command that instructs DOS to search through a specified set of directories for files with .COM, .EXE, and .BAT extensions. DOS searches this path if the selected command, executable, or batch file can't be found in the current directory.

117

The Directory Structure

DOS uses the directory to find files on a disk. The directory is held in computer format on the disk itself. The directory contains the file name, size, and creation or revision date information. Computer operators use the directory of a disk to find specific files. DOS also uses some or all of this directory information to efficiently service requests for data stored in the files on your disks.

All MS-DOS-based disks have at least one directory. One directory is usually adequate for a floppy disk. Because floppy disks have relatively limited capacities, the number of files you can store on a floppy is limited. Fixed disks, or hard disks, on the other hand, have relatively large capacities. A fixed disk can contain hundreds or even thousands of files. Without an organizational method, both DOS and you would have to sift and sort through all directory entries to find a specific file. Imagine issuing a DIR command that resulted in ten or twelve screens of file names, dates, and sizes!

Starting with version 2, MS-DOS incorporated a *hierarchical directory system*. This multi-level file structure lets you create a filing system for your many programs and files. Hierarchical directories are beneficial. You can store your disk files in smaller, more logically grouped directories so that you (and DOS) can locate those files.

Computer people use the term *tree structure* to refer to the organization of files into hierarchical levels of directories. Try picturing the tree structure as an inverted tree. You can visualize the file system with the first-level directory as the root or trunk of the tree. The trunk branches into major limbs to the next level of directories under the root. These directories branch into other directories. The directories have files, like leaves, attached to them. Directories below the root directory are called *subdirectories*. The terms *directory* and *subdirectory* are frequently used interchangeably, however.

At any time, you can work within a directory that is at any branch of the tree. By naming the branches, you can describe where you are working in the tree structure. You simply start at the root and name each branch that leads to your current branch.

When you prepare a disk for your computer, DOS creates one directory for that disk. This main directory is called the *root* directory. The root directory is the default directory until you change to another directory. DOS designates the root directory with the backslash (\) character. You cannot delete the root directory.

A subdirectory is any other directory besides the root directory. A subdirectory can contain data files as well as other, lower subdirectories. Subdirectory names must conform to the naming rules for DOS files, but subdirectory names normally do not have extensions. It is a good idea to name subdirectories for the type of files they contain. In this way, you can remember what type of files each subdirectory contains.

Directories do not share information about their contents with other directories. In a way, each subdirectory acts as a disk within a bigger disk. This idea of privacy extends to the DOS commands that you issue. The directory structure allows DOS commands to act upon the contents of the current directory and leave other directories undisturbed.

The directory you are working in is your default or current directory. When you issue a command that specifies a file but not a directory, DOS uses your current directory. You can access any point in the tree structure and remain at your current directory.

The Directory Structure

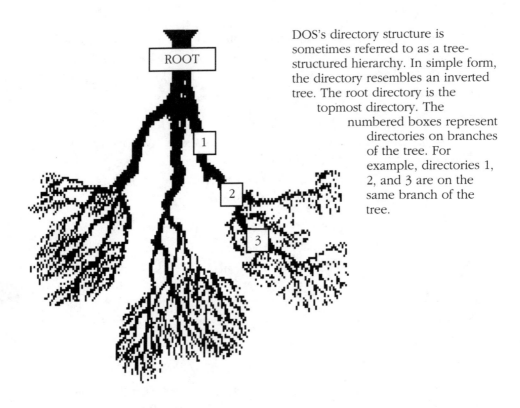

DOS's directory structure is sometimes referred to as a tree-structured hierarchy. In simple form, the directory resembles an inverted tree. The root directory is the topmost directory. The numbered boxes represent directories on branches of the tree. For example, directories 1, 2, and 3 are on the same branch of the tree.

The tree-structure analogy loses some of its neatness when it is expanded to cover the capabilities of the hierarchical directory structure. That is because any directory, except the root, can have as many subdirectories as space on the disk allows.

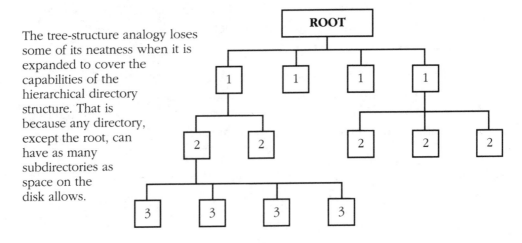

```
                    ┌─────────────────────────────┐
                    │     PARENT CORPORATION      │
                    └─────────────────────────────┘
                 ┌──────────────┴──────────────┐
         ┌───────────────┐            ┌───────────────┐
         │ Subsidiary 1  │            │ Subsidiary 1  │
         └───────────────┘            └───────────────┘
       ┌────────┼────────┐
   ┌───────┐ ┌───────┐ ┌───────┐
   │ Sub 2 │ │ Sub 2 │ │ Sub 2 │
   └───────┘ └───────┘ └───────┘
               ┌───────┐
               │ Sub 3 │
               └───────┘
```

Disk directories are frequently referred to as "parent" and "child" directories. This structure can be compared to that of a well-diversified corporation with numerous subsidiaries. Each "child" of the parent can have "children" of its own. In the directory hierarchy, each directory's "parent" is the directory just above it.

Paths in the Tree Structure

Before DOS can locate a file in the tree structure, it must know where to find the file. The *directory specifier* simply tells DOS in which directory a certain file resides. DOS must know the drive you want to use, the directory name, and the name of the file. In the command line, you type the disk drive, the directory name, and finally, the file name. DOS uses this information to find the file.

Path Names

A *path name* is a chain of directory names that tells DOS how to find the file you want. You type the drive name, a subdirectory name or sequence of subdirectory names, and the file name. You separate subdirectory names from each other with a *backslash* character (\). Using symbolic notation, the path name looks like this:

$d:\backslash directory\backslash directory. . .\backslash filename.ext$

In this notation, *d:* is the drive letter. If you omit the drive specifier, DOS uses the logged drive as the default drive. The *directory\backslash directory*. . . names the directory you want to search. The ellipsis (. . .) simply means that you could have other directories listed. If you omit the directory specifier from the path name, DOS assumes that the directory you want to use is the current directory. *filename.ext* is the name of the file. Notice that you use a \ to separate directory names and the file name. The path name fully describes to DOS where to direct its search for the file.

Where the Search Starts

When you type a path name, DOS searches in the first specified directory and passes through the other specified directory branches to the file. The root directory has no name and is represented by the backslash (\). All directories grow from the root directory. If you want the search path to start at the root directory, begin the directory specification with a \. DOS will begin its search for the file in the root and follow the subdirectory chain you include in the command.

Suppose that you wanted to check the size of a budget file created by your Lotus 1-2-3 program. You might use a DIR command, giving DOS a path something like the following to search:

DIR C:\LOTUS\DATA\BUDGET.WKS

DOS will search on drive C, beginning with the root directory and proceeding to the LOTUS subdirectory and then to the DATA subdirectory. If you omit the \ root name designator, DOS will search for files in your current directory and in subdirectories of your current directory. The search will start in your current directory, not the root directory. DOS uses the path to your current directory as its default. If the current directory does not lead to the subdirectory that contains the file, this method will not work. However, if the current directory contains the subdirectory, you do not have to type all the directory names in the path. In the preceding example, the current directory was C:\LOTUS. You can get the size of the budget file with the following command:

DIR DATA\BUDGET.WKS

123

Paths in the Tree Structure

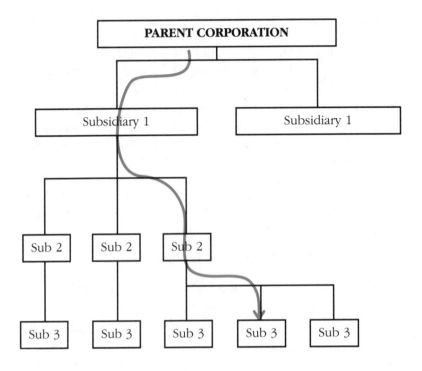

You can compare DOS to a corporate empire that has an extremely strict order of command. All communications must "go through channels." Thus, if a subsidiary at level 3 wants to communicate with the parent corporation, the message must go through both subsidiary 2 and 1. In DOS, this routing is called the *path*.

Introduction

The Directory
Structure

**Paths in the
Tree Structure**

Sample
Subdirectory
Setups

Hierarchical
Directory
Commands

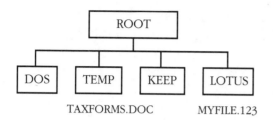

Use this simple directory setup to understand the concept of directory paths in DOS. Each subdirectory in this sample is a subdirectory of the root directory. One subdirectory, LOTUS, has a data file, MYFILE.123. Another subdirectory, \TEMP, has a file called TAXFORMS.DOC.

Path Names

MYFILE.123 is a data file in the LOTUS subdirectory. The complete path name for this file is the chain of directories that tells DOS how to find MYFILE.123. In this case, the chain consists of just two directories: the root (\) and \LOTUS. The path name is

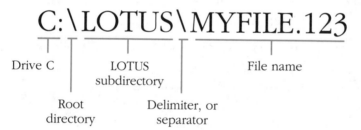

The path name for the TAXFORMS.DOC file is

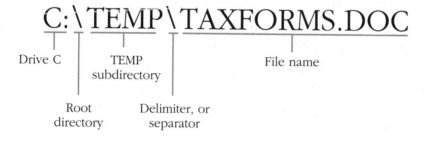

Sample Subdirectory Setups

Although you may not know what kind of directory organization you need, now is a good time to give some thought to establishing your directory tree. If your computer is part of a network, check with the network administrator before you make any changes.

The Root Directory

DOS creates the root directory for you, but you control which files to include in the root. The root is the top directory in the inverted tree, and therefore, you should avoid cluttering the root directory with files. Because the root is the default directory for DOS when you boot your system, you should include COMMAND.COM. in the root directory. DOS expects to find COMMAND.COM in the current directory when you boot. If DOS cannot load COMMAND.COM, DOS cannot communicate with you. DOS only manages to warn you that it cannot find the command interpreter.

In addition to COMMAND.COM, the root directory will likely contain the AUTOEXEC.BAT and CONFIG.SYS files. You will learn about these files in Chapter 10. The AUTOEXEC.BAT file usually contains the PATH command that sets the search paths automatically. The root also contains the primary subdirectories for your computer. If your disk has no subdirectories, you will add the first one to the root directory.

The \DOS Directory

You should create a \DOS directory and include it in your PATH command. All the utility files from your original DOS disks should be copied into this directory. You will then have all of your DOS functions grouped into one directory.

\TEMP

Many users find they need a directory to store temporary files. You might find a directory named \TEMP useful. You can copy files to \TEMP as a temporary storage place until you copy the files to a more appropriate directory. A \TEMP directory is also useful for making copies of floppies in a single floppy, low-memory system. You can copy files from the source disk to the \TEMP directory and then copy back to the destination disk. If you have a single floppy drive, this copy method keeps you from swapping disks in and out of the single floppy drive.

Do not use the \TEMP directory as a permanent home for a file, however. You should be able to use a wild card to erase the directory periodically. This keeps the \TEMP directory clean for subsequent use.

\MISC or \KEEP

You may have files in different directories that are no longer active, but that you feel you may still need. Inactive files in a directory tend to increase clutter and make sorting through the directory confusing. With a \MISC or a \KEEP directory, you can have an easy-to-remember home for those inactive files. Of course, you should only delete those files that are obviously of no more use to you.

Applications Software Directories

Many applications packages create directories when you install them on your hard disk. If they do not, it's a good idea to create a directory with a name that conveys the package name. You can then copy the package's files to the directory.

Sample Subdirectory Setups

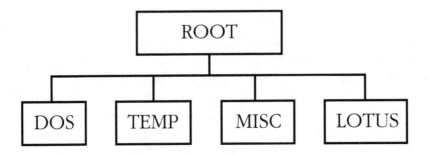

This diagram and screen show the structure of a simple directory system. The structure consists of four subdirectories, each a subdirectory of the root directory.

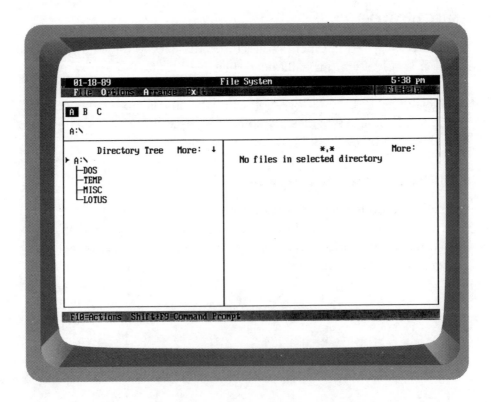

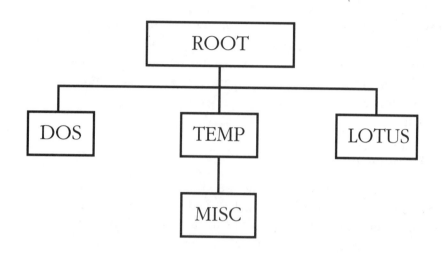

A variety of arrangements for the directory structure is possible. Many users find that two levels of subdirectories are sufficient.

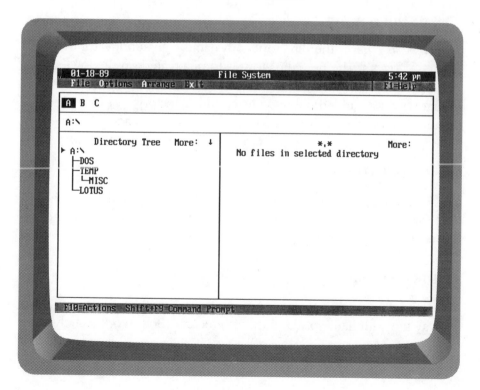

Hierarchical Directory Commands

The examples presented so far in this chapter provide information on the structure of hierarchical directories. Now you will learn commands that relate to your directory system's maintenance and use. These DOS commands consist of the command name and parameters. With directory commands, you can customize your file system and navigate through it.

MKDIR Command

To add a directory to your disk, use the MKDIR command. This command name has two names: MKDIR and MD. The command names are interchangeable. MKDIR means MaKe DIRectory. MD is an abbreviated name for the make directory command. Decide upon a name for your proposed new directory and use the MKDIR command at the DOS prompt in the form

MKDIR *directory specifier*

Directory specifier is the directory path name with subdirectories separated by \'s. The new directory is to be created on the logged drive by default. If you omit the leading \ in your path, then the new directory will be added below your current directory. For example, assume that drive C is the logged drive. You want to add a directory called TEMP to hold files temporarily. At the DOS prompt, enter

MKDIR \TEMP

Press the Enter key. DOS creates the TEMP directory directly under the root directory (\). You can use the DIR command to verify that the TEMP directory exists.

CHDIR Command

Use the CHDIR or CD command to change to another directory or to display the path name of the current directory. Both work exactly alike. The CD command changes your position in the tree structure of directories. Decide which subdirectory you want as a working directory. Issue the command at the DOS prompt in the form

> **CD** *directory specifier*

Directory specifier is the path name of the directory that you want to change to. Notice that the CD command has the same form as the MKDIR command. To change to the TEMP directory of the preceding example, enter the command

> **CD \TEMP**

You can confirm that DOS changed your working directory to \TEMP. Just issue the CD command with no parameters and DOS will display the current directory's path name. CD is an important command for DOS beginners. You can use CD to change to a directory from which you want information. Whenever you are positioned in the directory that holds the commands or data you need to use, you can omit the directory name from the command line. When you issue the CD command, the directory you change to becomes the default directory.

RMDIR Command

You use the RMDIR or RD command to remove (delete) directories when you no longer need them. The command names RMDIR and RD work exactly alike. Before you remove a directory, the directory must be empty of all files and subdirectories. You cannot delete your current working directory. If you want to delete your working directory, you must first change to another directory and delete all the files from the unwanted directory. The directory you change must not contain the directory you want to delete as part of its path name for the RMDIR to work.

Hierarchical Directory Commands

To remove a directory from the logged drive, issue the RMDIR command at the DOS prompt in the form

RMDIR *directory pathname*

To delete the TEMP directory used in the examples, you issue the command as

RMDIR \TEMP

PATH command

If the file for the command you want DOS to execute is not in the current directory, you must give DOS the correct *path*. The PATH command instructs DOS to use a certain route to find files. Most often, you will use the PATH command to find an external DOS command. COMMAND.COM also uses the PATH command to find and start programs that are not in the current directory.

DOS retains the PATH until you change the command or reboot the computer. If you include more than one directory path in the command, you must separate the paths with a semicolon (;) character. To issue the PATH command for the logged drive, at the DOS prompt type

PATH *d:path specifier;d:path specifier;...*

The drive specifier *d:* names the drive on which DOS is to search. The first *path specifier* is the first alternative search path. The semicolon (;) separates the first search path from the optional second path. The ellipsis simply means that you can have other path specifiers in your command line.

You can create a \DOS directory to store the DOS utility files. You then issue the path command:

PATH C:\DOS

Once this PATH command is issued, whenever you use an external DOS command in a directory other than \DOS, the PATH specification leads COMMAND.COM to the command's program file in the \DOS directory.

TREE Command

When you add many directories to your disk, you may lose track of the directory names and what files they contain. You can keep track of the organization of the directory with the TREE command.

You can use TREE to display all directory paths on the logged disk, and as an option, each directory's files. To list all directories, issue the TREE command at the DOS prompt in the form:

TREE \ /F

/F is an optional switch. It tells DOS to list the file names in the listing of directories. If the output information is too much for one screen, you can stop the scrolling with the Ctrl-S key sequence. You restart the scrolling by pressing any key. You can get a print out of the results of the TREE command. Chapter 9 will show you how to redirect a command's output to your printer or to a file.

Hierarchical Directory Commands

MD MKDIR	*Makes* a directory.
CD CHDIR	Shows the path of or *changes* the current directory.
RD RMDIR	*Removes* a directory.

Making Directories and Viewing Their Contents

```
C>CD                    Shows current directory

C>C:\                   Current directory is the root
                        directory (\)

C>MKDIR \TEMP   Makes a new directory called TEMP

C>CD \TEMP      Changes current directory to TEMP

C>DIR           Displays contents of the TEMP directory


Volume in drive C has no label
Volume Serial Number is 146E-3CA4
Directory of C:\TEMP
.        <DIR> 12-20-88  3:45p
..       <DIR> 12-20-88  3:45p
2 File(s)   3956736 bytes free
```

```
CD                    Shows current directory
C:\TEMP               Current directory is TEMP

C>CD\                 Changes current directory to root (\)

C>MD \MISC            Makes a directory called MISC

C>CD \MISC            Changes current directory to MISC

C>DIR                 Displays contents of MISC directory


Volume in drive C has no label
Volume Serial Number is 146E-3CA4
Directory of C:\TEMP
.        <DIR> 12-20-88  3:46p
..       <DIR> 12-20-88  3:46p
2 File(s)   3954688 bytes free
```

The last line of the directory listing indicates the number of files in the directory. Both TEMP and MISC are empty, except for two files created by DOS. The period (.) is DOS's shorthand for the current directory. The double period (..) represents the parent of the current directory.

Hierarchical Directory Commands

Making A Subdirectory of a Subdirectory

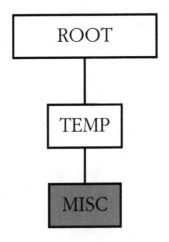

This directory structure shows how new directory branches were added to the hierarchical file-structure tree.

To make a directory anywhere in the file system, use the MKDIR command with the full path name of the new directory. The leading backslash shows the path from the root.

Notice that only the new directory name needs to be specified to create the MISC subdirectory below \TEMP. This is so because \TEMP is the current directory. The MISC subdirectory could have been created from anywhere within the file system by using the command MKDIR \TEMP\MISC.

```
C>CD \TEMP

C>CD

C:\TEMP

C>MD MISC

C>DIR

Volume in drive C has no label
Volume Serial Number is XXXX-XXXX
Directory of C:\TEMP
.          <DIR>  12-20-88    4:45p
..         <DIR>  12-20-88    4:45p
MISC       <DIR>  01-11-89    2:02p
3 File(s)        3356672 bytes free
```

This screen shows that the current directory is \TEMP. To create a subdirectory called MISC under \TEMP, issue the command **MKDIR MISC.**

Removing a Directory

```
C> CD MISC

C>RMDIR MISC

Attempt to remove current
directory - \MISC

C>CD

C:\TEMP\MISC
```

This command changes you to the \TEMP\MISC subdirectory because \TEMP is the current directory.

The usual reason you get error messages when you use hierarchical directory commands is that you are not where you think you are in the hierarchical directory structure. The CD command lets you know where you are.

```
C>CD\

C>RMDIR MISC

Invalid path, not directory, or
directory not empty.
```

The RMDIR MISC command generates an error message because of the way it was issued. MISC is not a subdirectory of the current directory, which is the root, and DOS could not find the path to the MISC subdirectory from the root. The error in this case was an invalid path. You will also get this message if a directory contains any files except . and ..You do not have to erase these files to remove a directory.

```
C>CD \TEMP

C>RMDIR MISC

C>
```

\TEMP is the current directory. From it, you can erase the empty subdirectory MISC.

137

Hierarchical Directory Commands

The PATH Command

DOS knows how to find external command files in three situations:

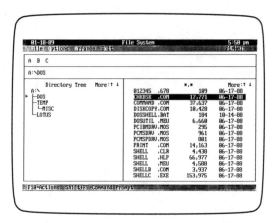

(1) The file is in the current directory in which you are working.

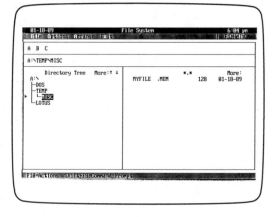

(2) The file is not in the current directory, but you include the full path on the command line:
C:\DOS\CHKDSK A:.

(3) The directory in which the file is located is on the search path established by the PATH command. This PATH command instructs DOS to search each directory shown:

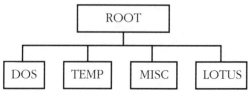

PATH=C:\DOS;C:\TEMP;C:\MISC;C:\LOTUS;C:\;

The TREE Command

TREE's output helps you keep track of your disk's organization.

```
A>TREE
Directory PATH listing
Volume Serial Number is 2F3C-18C5
A:,
├───DOS
├───TEMP
│   └───MISC
└───LOTUS

A>
```

```
A>TREE/F
Directory PATH listing
Volume Serial Number is 2F3C-18C5
A:,
├───DOS
│       COMMAND.COM
│       CHKDSK.COM
│       DISKCOPY.COM
│       PRINT.COM
│       SHELL.CLR
│       SHELL.HLP
│       SHELL.MEU
│       SHELLB.COM
│       SHELLC.EXE
│       DOSUTIL.MEU
│       012345.678
│       DOSSHELL.BAT
│
├───TEMP
│   └───MISC
│           MYFILE.MEM
│
└───LOTUS

A>
```

139

7

Copying and Deleting Files

Disk files are the primary storage place for data and programs. A knowledge of how to manage these files is essential. If you want to be in control of your work, you must be in control of your files. This chapter tells you how to copy disks and files, how to erase unneeded files, and how to rename existing files.

When you work with floppy disks, always keep the labels on your disks accurate. Use a felt-tipped pen and indicate the contents on the disk label as you work. Disks not labeled or labeled inaccurately are an invitation to lost data. If you do not label disks, you may mistake them for blank unformatted disks.

Key Terms Used in This Chapter

Source   The disk or file from which you are copying.

Destination   The disk or file to which you are copying.

Target   Same as destination.

Fragmentation   The condition that results when a disk file is contained in sectors that are not contiguous because of adding and deleting files.

Current directory   The directory that DOS uses as the default directory. The root directory is the current directory on the logged drive until you change to another directory with the CHDIR (CD) command.

Overwrite   Writing new information over old in a disk file.

Copying and Comparing Disks

The DISKCOPY command makes an exact copy of another disk. DISKCOPY reads the input, or *source,* disk and then writes the data to another disk, the *destination* disk. DISKCOPY is good to use when you want to make a working copy of a master disk. You then can store the master disk in a safe place. DISKCOPY also copies the system files from a bootable source disk to make a copy that is bootable.

In this chapter, you will learn a simple form of the DISKCOPY command. The basic DISKCOPY command assumes that your source and destination disks are the same size and capacity. You may find another Que title, *MS-DOS User's Guide,* 3rd Ed., helpful if you need more information on DISKCOPY.

The DISKCOPY Command

DISKCOPY is an external command that you load from disk. You must have the disk that contains DISKCOPY in your default drive or set the correct path with the PATH command (see Chapter 6). Use the DISKCOPY command to copy floppies only. The correct syntax for DISKCOPY is

> **DISKCOPY** *source d: destination d:*

The *source d:* is the name for the drive that holds the disk that you want to copy. The *destination d:* is the name of the drive that holds the disk to receive the copy. As always, type a colon after the drive name. Insert a space between the source and destination drive names. If you use a blank disk as the destination disk, DOS first formats it. An example of the command is

> **DISKCOPY A: B:**

After you issue the DISKCOPY command, DOS prompts you to put the disks into the proper drives. Make sure that you put them in the correct drives. If you write-protect the source disk, you safeguard its contents in case of a mix-up. Strike a key and the copy process will begin. When the copy process finishes, DOS asks if you want to make another copy. Answer **Y** or **N**. You can make another copy at this time. If you answer Y, you do not have to access DISKCOPY again because DOS has the program in memory.

If you leave out the drive names in the DISKCOPY command line, DOS uses the default drive as the specifier. To avoid confusion, always give both the source and destination drive names.

Comparing Disks with DISKCOMP

You can confirm that two disks are identical by using the external DISKCOMP command. DISKCOMP compares disks sector by sector. Remember that the disks and capacities must be the same for both disks in the comparison. Any difference in disks made with DISKCOPY is a sign of a problem disk. Issue the command in the form

DISKCOMP *source d: destination d:*

Notice that the syntax for DISKCOMP is like the syntax for DISKCOPY. Load the two disks at the prompt, and DOS will confirm the comparison or point out the differences. As with DISKCOPY, you can repeat the DISKCOMP command. An example of the DISKCOMP command is

DISKCOMP A: B:

Again, if you omit a drive designator, DOS uses the default drive.

Copying and Comparing Disks

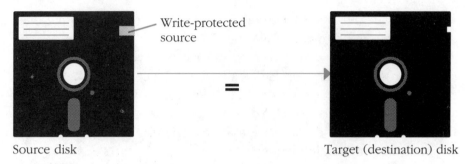

Write-protected source

Source disk   Target (destination) disk

The DISKCOPY command makes an exact copy of another disk. DISKCOPY requires that the source and destination disks be the same size and capacity.

```
A>DISKCOPY A: B:

Insert SOURCE diskette in drive A:

Insert TARGET diskette in drive B:

Press any key to continue . . .

Copying 40 tracks
9 Sectors/Track, 2 Side(s)

Copy another diskette (Y/N)? N

A>
```

The common syntax for DISKCOPY is DISKCOPY A: B:. DOS prompts you to insert the disks before the copy begins.

If drives or disks are not compatible, you will get an error message, and no copy will take place.

```
A>DISKCOPY A: B:

Drive types or diskette types
not compatible

A>
```

Write-protected
source

Source disk   Target (destination) disk

If the DISKCOPY command is issued with no drive parameters, DOS will copy
using just one drive. DOS will prompt you to alternately switch between
inserting the source and destination disks. Depending on your system's
memory, you will swap disks once or several times.

```
A>DISKCOPY
```

By entering
DISKCOPY alone,
you are telling DOS
to use one drive.
Make sure you
don't get the disks
confused during
swapping.

Copying and Comparing Disks

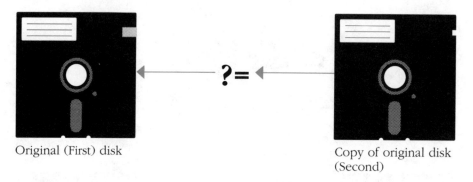

Original (First) disk

Copy of original disk
(Second)

The DISKCOMP command compares two disks of equal size and capacity to
confirm that both are the same. Normally, you use DISKCOMP to test disks
that were made from originals using the DISKCOPY command. If the disks
compare, DOS gives the message Compare OK.

```
A>DISKCOMP A: B:

Insert FIRST diskette in drive A:

Insert SECOND diskette in drive B:

Press any key to continue . . .

Comparing 40 tracks
9 sectors per track, 2 side(s)

Compare error on
side 0, track 0

Compare error on
side 0, track 3

Compare another diskette (Y/N) ?N

A>
```

In this example, a working
copy of a master disk is
compared to the master.
Notice the compare errors.
The working copy is no
longer reliable, or other files
have been added to the disk
since it was DISKCOPYed
from the master. To solve the
problem, the best bet would
be to make a new working
copy.

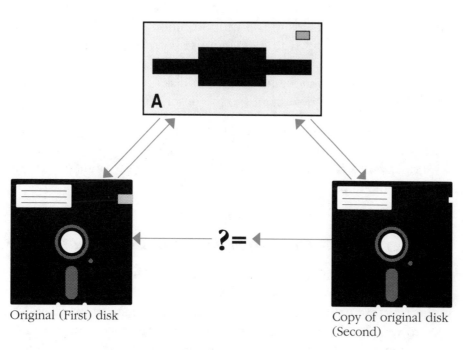

Original (First) disk | Copy of original disk (Second)

If the DISKCOMP command is issued with no drive parameters, DOS will carry out the comparison using just one drive. DOS will alternately prompt you to switch between inserting the first and second disks. Depending on your system's memory, you will swap disks once or several times.

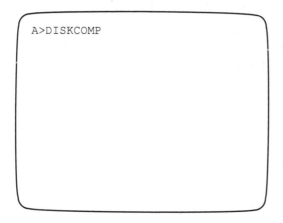

```
A>DISKCOMP
```

By entering DISKCOMP alone, you are telling DOS to use one drive. Make sure you don't get the disks confused during swapping.

Copying Files with COPY

The internal COPY command is a DOS workhorse. DISKCOPY works with disks; COPY works with files. Because copy is an internal command, you can issue the command any time at the DOS prompt. You can use COPY to move files between disks of different sizes and capacities and to give new names to the destination files.

COPY is a versatile command that allows wild cards in the syntax. To teach you every use of the COPY command would be a large job. In this book, you will learn the COPY command that you are likely to use in daily computing.

The symbolic syntax of the copy command is

COPY *sd:\path\filename.ext dd:\path\filename.ext* /V

The **sd:** is the source file's drive name and *dd:* is the destination file's drive name. The **\path\filename.ext** is the full path name for the file in the directory tree structure. The **/V** is an optional switch that tells DOS to verify that the copy is correct. A delimiting space separates the source and destination parts of the command. An example of the full COPY command is

COPY C:\MISC\MYFILE.MEM A:\KEEP\MYFILE.KEP /V

MYFILE.MEM is a file located on drive C in the \MISC directory. MYFILE.MEM is copied to a new file named MYFILE.KEP in the \KEEP directory on drive A. In this example, you might omit some of the items of syntax without disturbing the copying process because of defaults.

Introduction

Copying and
Comparing Disks

**Copying Files
with COPY**

Deleting and
Renaming Files

You learned about default values in earlier chapters, but you also need to understand how DOS handles defaults in copy commands. The *rule of currents* states that if you do not specify one of the drives in the copy command, DOS will use the current (default or logged) drive. If you do not specify a path in the command, DOS will use the current directory of the disk in question. If you do not specify a destination file name, the copied file keeps the current file name of the source file. You will see how the rule of currents applies to COPY in later examples.

If you give a disk drive and path for the source file, but omit the file name, DOS assumes that you want to copy *all* files in the directory. This assumption is equivalent to using the wild card *.* as the file specifier for the source file.

COPY can be a dangerous command because it overwrites files on the destination disk whose names duplicate names on the source disk. Always check directories for duplicate file names before you try copying files. It is also easy to confuse disk drives. You can easily copy old versions over new file versions. The use of wild cards in file names can also be the source of regrettable results. Just remember that COPY does what you instruct it to do. Make sure that you do not tell COPY to do something you don't want it to do.

If you are uncertain about COPY syntax, you can write-protect your source disk if it is a floppy. Keep the rule of currents in mind, and you can customize the examples to do almost any file copying job.

Copying Files with COPY

Copying All Files in a Directory

As you add and delete files from a disk, the free space for new file information becomes physically spread around the surface of the disk. This phenomenon is called *fragmentation*. DOS allocates data storage space by finding the next available disk space. If the next available space is too small to hold an entire file, DOS uses all of that space and puts the rest of the file into the next available space(s). Fragmented files lower disk performance.

If you use DISKCOPY on a fragmented floppy disk, you get an exact image of the fragmented disk. To avoid copying fragmentation, or to make an efficient copy of a fragmented floppy disk, use the COPY command. First, format the destination disk and make sure that the disk contains enough room to hold all of the source files. Then copy the source files to the destination disk with no fragmentation. To do so, place the source disk in drive A and the destination disk in drive B and type

COPY A:*.* B:

In this example, you copied all of the files on the disk in drive A to the disk in drive B, keeping the same file names. (Remember the rule of currents.) By changing to a directory on your hard disk, you can copy all of the files of the last example to that directory by using C: in place of B:. If you want the destination disk to be bootable, format it with the /S switch first. You cannot, however, use the COPY command to copy DOS's hidden system files.

Copying Single or Multiple files from Disk to Disk

You can copy one file or many files to another disk for safe keeping, to move data to another computer, or for any other purpose. Simply use the COPY command with a file name or a wild card that matches the file(s) you want to move to the other disk. Put the disk with the source file(s) in drive A. Put the destination disk in drive B. Type **DIR A:** to see and calculate the size of the file(s) you want to copy. Then type **DIR B:** to see if the destination disk contains sufficient free space. If sufficient space is on the destination disk, enter the COPY command. An example command is

COPY A:*.DOC B:/V

In this example, DOS copies all files with the extension DOC to the disk in drive B and verifies the copy. The destination file name was omitted. DOS accepts the original names by default unless you tell it otherwise. You can omit the name of your logged drive from this example, but to be on the safe side, you should include it.

To copy one file from the source disk to a different destination disk you might enter

COPY A:SPEECH.DOC B:/V

This command copies the SPEECH.DOC file from the disk in drive A to the disk in drive B. Again, the name remains the same. If you have a hard disk, you can use a command like this:

COPY A:SPEECH.DOC C:/V

151

Copying Files with COPY

This command line copies the SPEECH file from the floppy disk in drive A to the current directory of the hard disk. Similarly, you can copy from your current hard disk directory to a floppy disk:

COPY SPEECH.DOC A:

DOS finds the SPEECH file in the current directory of the logged C drive and copies it with the same name to the floppy disk in drive A.

Copying a File to the Same Disk Directory

You often may want to place a duplicate copy of a file on the same disk. (For this example, you can assume that floppy disks have only a root directory.) You cannot have duplicate file names and extensions in one directory. You also cannot copy a file onto itself. To copy the file into the same directory, you must give it another name, another extension, or both. Most people give the file a different extension and keep the file name the same.

To duplicate a file and place it in the same directory, you must enter a source file name and a destination file name in the command line. Change to the drive and directory that holds the file that you want to duplicate and type:

COPY SPEECH.DOC SPEECH.BAK

In this example, you used the rule of currents. Because you did not specify a drive, DOS used the default drive. You now have a duplicate copy of SPEECH.DOC, named SPEECH.BAK. By using the BAK extension, you can recognize the new file as a backup of the original file. You also might give the destination file a completely new name. In this example, you can list both files with the command

DIR SPEECH.*

Copying a File across Directories

If you have a hard disk, you need a method of copying files from one directory to another. For this use of COPY, assume that you are in the directory that contains the source file(s) and that you have created the destination directory. Although this discussion of COPY can apply to floppies with subdirectories, users of hard disks are the ones most likely encounter this situation.

You can have duplicate file names and extensions in *different* directories; therefore, you can omit the destination file name for this example. Because your current directory is the one that contains the source file, you can omit the source path. The correct syntax is

COPY SPEECH.DOC \MISC /V

This command copies the file SPEECH.DOC from the current drive and directory. You now have SPEECH.DOC in the subdirectory \MISC on the current drive. The command also verifies the copy.

When you copy files between subdirectories, the DOS CD command is useful. Using CD with a directory name changes the default directory. You can verify your location by using the CD command with no parameters. Use CD to change the current directory to the source file's directory. You can then take advantage of the rule of currents by omitting the source file's drive and path names in the command.

153

Copying Files with COPY

The copy command has many variations. Yet every copy command copies from a source to a destination. DOS uses the following items to determine the source and destination:

Disk drives

Path

\DIRECT1

\DIRECT2

File name and extension

FILE.EXT	*.EXT	FILE.*	*.*
Full File Name	Wild Card File Name	Wild Card Extension	Full Wild Card

A>COPY C:\MISC\MYFILE.MEM A:\KEEP\MYFILE.KEP

Source   Destination

In the full form of COPY, the drive, the path, and the file name and extension are given for both the source and destination files. The full form of COPY can be used for every COPY command if you want.

```
A>C:

C>

C>CD\TEMP

C>CD

C:\TEMP
```

If either the source or
destination path is the current
path, the path name may be
omitted. A path (directory) is
made current by issuing the
CD command, naming the
directory to be made current.
The CD command with no
parameters shows the current
directory path.

Wild cards (? and *) can be used in the file name and extension to allow the
COPY command to match source files and copy them to destination files. The
power of copying multiple files with wild cards is a good reason to choose file
names that lend themselves to matching with wild cards.

```
COPY *.DOC will copy

FILE1.DOC

FILE2.DOC

FILE3.DOC
```

If the destination file name is
omitted, DOS uses the source
file name as the name for the
new, copied file:

Typed command:

  COPY A:samename.fil B:

What DOS knows by the rule
of currents:

  samename.fil

Copying Files with COPY

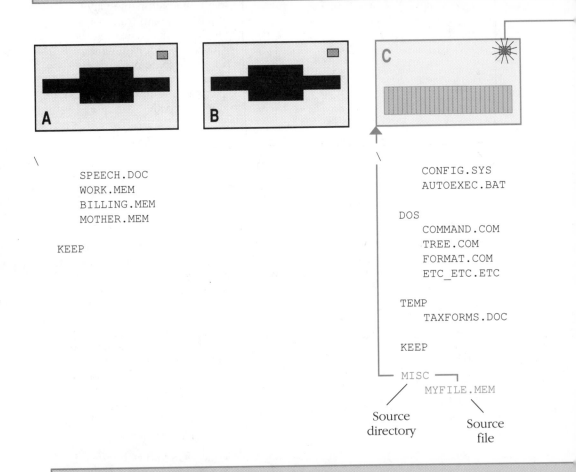

Command as issued:

COPY C:\MISC\MYFILE.MEM A:\KEEP\MYFILE.KEP/V

A

B

C

\

```
SPEECH.DOC
WORK.MEM
BILLING.MEM
MOTHER.MEM

KEEP
```

\

```
            CONFIG.SYS
            AUTOEXEC.BAT

DOS
    COMMAND.COM
    TREE.COM
    FORMAT.COM
    ETC_ETC.ETC

TEMP
    TAXFORMS.DOC

KEEP

MISC
    MYFILE.MEM
```

Source
directory

Source
file

In this version of COPY, the full form of COPY is used. The command gives DOS all the parameters needed to locate and copy a file from the directory tree of the source drive to the directory and file name of the destination.

What DOS knows by the rule of currents: Every parameter that DOS needs is available with this full version of the command.

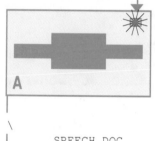

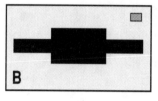

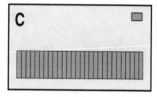

```
\
   SPEECH.DOC
   WORK.MEM
   BILLING.MEM
   MOTHER.MEM

KEEP
   MYFILE.KEP
```

Destination
directory

Destination
file

```
\
        CONFIG.SYS
        AUTOEXEC.BAT

DOS
        COMMAND.COM
        TREE.COM
        FORMAT.COM
        ETC_ETC.ETC

TEMP
        TAXFORMS.DOC

KEEP

MISC
        MYFILE.MEM
```

The /V at the end of the command is a switch that tells DOS to verify the copied file after the copy is made. The full version of COPY does not rely on DOS's current default drive or directory.

157

Copying Files with COPY

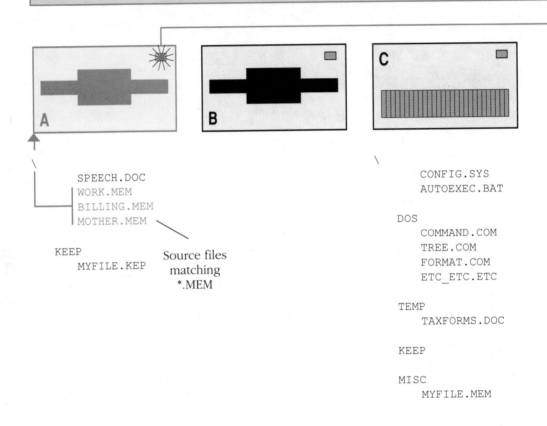

```
\
        SPEECH.DOC
        WORK.MEM
        BILLING.MEM
        MOTHER.MEM

    KEEP
        MYFILE.KEP
```

Source files
matching
*.MEM

```
\
        CONFIG.SYS
        AUTOEXEC.BAT

    DOS
        COMMAND.COM
        TREE.COM
        FORMAT.COM
        ETC_ETC.ETC

    TEMP
        TAXFORMS.DOC

    KEEP

    MISC
        MYFILE.MEM
```

This example of COPY copies multiple files from disk to disk. In this case, the working current directory of both the disk in drive A and the disk in drive B is \ (the root directory). Since both root directories are current on their disk, DOS knows the path specifier, and you may omit it in both the source and

What DOS knows by the rule of currents: COPY A:*.MEM B:*.MEM

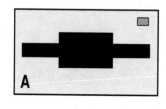

```
\
        SPEECH.DOC
        WORK.MEM
        BILLING.MEM
        MOTHER.MEM

KEEP
        MYFILE.KEP
```

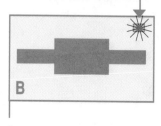

```
\
        WORK.MEM
        BILLING.MEM
        MOTHER.MEM
```

Destination
files given the
same names as
the source files

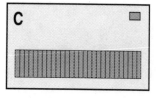

```
\
        CONFIG.SYS
        AUTOEXEC.BAT

DOS
        COMMAND.COM
        TREE.COM
        FORMAT.COM
        ETC_ETC.ETC

TEMP
        TAXFORMS.DOC

KEEP

MISC
        MYFILE.MEM
```

destination. The source filename *.MEM tells DOS to copy any file from the
source directory that matches the MEM extension. Since the destination file
name and extension are omitted, DOS uses the filenames of the source files
for the copy.

159

Copying Files with COPY

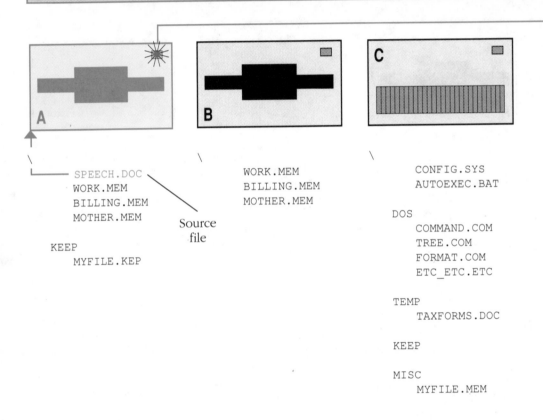

```
\
    SPEECH.DOC
  WORK.MEM
  BILLING.MEM
  MOTHER.MEM

 KEEP
    MYFILE.KEP
```

Source
file

```
\
  WORK.MEM
  BILLING.MEM
  MOTHER.MEM
```

```
\
    CONFIG.SYS
    AUTOEXEC.BAT

DOS
    COMMAND.COM
    TREE.COM
    FORMAT.COM
    ETC_ETC.ETC

TEMP
    TAXFORMS.DOC

KEEP

MISC
    MYFILE.MEM
```

This example of COPY copies one file from disk to disk. The root directories of the two disks are current and can be omitted from the command. Since the

160

What DOS knows by the rule of currents:
COPY A:\SPEECH.DOC B:\SPEECH.DOC/V

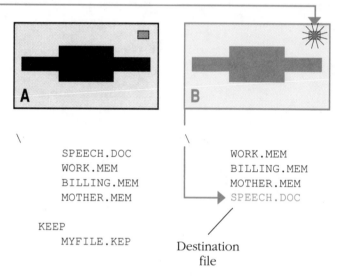

```
\

    SPEECH.DOC
    WORK.MEM
    BILLING.MEM
    MOTHER.MEM

KEEP
    MYFILE.KEP
```

```
\

    WORK.MEM
    BILLING.MEM
    MOTHER.MEM
    SPEECH.DOC
```

Destination file

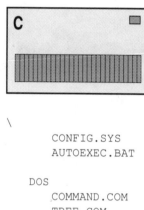

```
\

    CONFIG.SYS
    AUTOEXEC.BAT

DOS
    COMMAND.COM
    TREE.COM
    FORMAT.COM
    ETC_ETC.ETC

TEMP
    TAXFORMS.DOC

KEEP

MISC
    MYFILE.MEM
```

destination file name is omitted, the copied file will have the same name and extension as the source file. The /V switch verifies the copy.

161

Copying Files with COPY

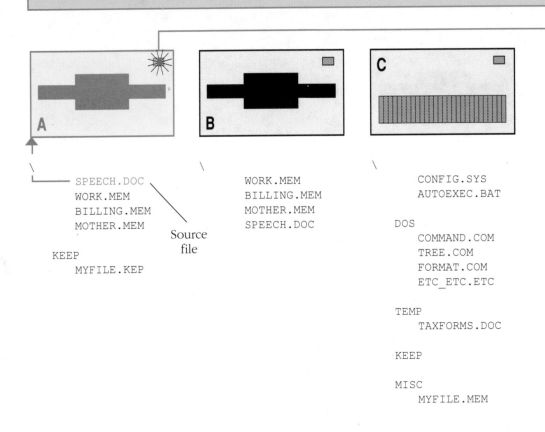

```
\                              \                    \
     SPEECH.DOC           WORK.MEM              CONFIG.SYS
     WORK.MEM             BILLING.MEM           AUTOEXEC.BAT
     BILLING.MEM          MOTHER.MEM
     MOTHER.MEM           SPEECH.DOC        DOS
                                               COMMAND.COM
  KEEP                                         TREE.COM
     MYFILE.KEP                                FORMAT.COM
                                               ETC_ETC.ETC

                                            TEMP
                                               TAXFORMS.DOC

                                            KEEP

                                            MISC
                                               MYFILE.MEM
```

Source
file

In this example of COPY, the directory \KEEP was made current on drive C with a CD\KEEP command. This is a floppy disk to hard disk copy where the path specifiers for the source and destination drives are omitted. The

What DOS knows by the rule of currents:
COPY A:\SPEECH.DOC C:\KEEP\SPEECH.DOC/V

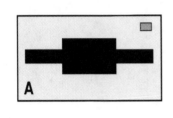

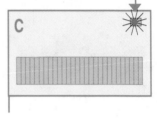

```
A
\
    SPEECH.DOC
    WORK.MEM
    BILLING.MEM
    MOTHER.MEM

  KEEP
    MYFILE.KEP
```

```
B
\
    WORK.MEM
    BILLING.MEM
    MOTHER.MEM
    SPEECH.DOC
```

```
C
\
    CONFIG.SYS
    AUTOEXEC.BAT

  DOS
    COMMAND.COM
    TREE.COM
    FORMAT.COM
    ETC_ETC.ETC

  TEMP
    TAXFORMS.DOC

  KEEP
    SPEECH.DOC

  MISC
    MYFILE.MEM
```

Destination path (directory)

Destination file

destination file name is omitted also. Again, since DOS knows the omitted parameters as its current defaults, the copy is made. The /V switch verifies the copy.

Copying Files with COPY

Command as issued:

   COPY SPEECH.DOC SPEECH.BAK

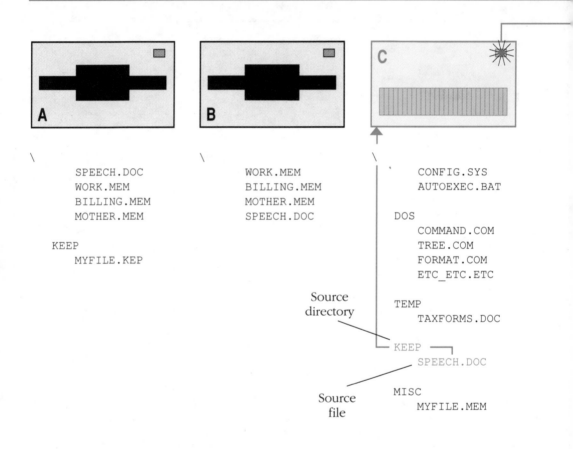

```
A                          B                          C

\                          \                          \
    SPEECH.DOC                 WORK.MEM                       CONFIG.SYS
    WORK.MEM                   BILLING.MEM                    AUTOEXEC.BAT
    BILLING.MEM                MOTHER.MEM
    MOTHER.MEM                 SPEECH.DOC                 DOS
                                                              COMMAND.COM
KEEP                                                          TREE.COM
    MYFILE.KEP                                                FORMAT.COM
                                                              ETC_ETC.ETC
```

```
                                                          TEMP
                                                              TAXFORMS.DOC

Source
directory                                                 KEEP
                                                              SPEECH.DOC

Source                                                    MISC
file                                                          MYFILE.MEM
```

In this example of COPY, a file is copied from and to the same directory on the same disk. The current drive is C, and the current directory is \KEEP. Since DOS will not allow duplicate file names in the same directory of the same disk, the extension of the destination file name has been changed. After the

What DOS knows by the rule of currents:
COPY C:\KEEP\SPEECH.DOC C:\KEEP\SPEECH.BAK

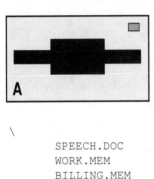

```
\
      SPEECH.DOC
      WORK.MEM
      BILLING.MEM
      MOTHER.MEM

   KEEP
      MYFILE.KEP
```

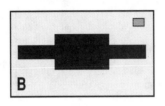

```
\
   WORK.MEM
   BILLING.MEM
   MOTHER.MEM
   SPEECH.DOC
```

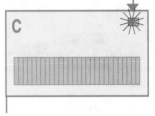

```
\
      CONFIG.SYS
      AUTOEXEC.BAT

   DOS
      COMMAND.COM
      TREE.COM
      FORMAT.COM
      ETC_ETC.ETC

   TEMP
      TAXFORMS.DOC

   KEEP
      SPEECH.DOC
      SPEECH.BAK

   MISC
      MYFILE.MEM
```

Destination directory

Destination file

copy, the two files will contain the same information (as with any copy). This form of copy is good for preserving a copy of a file in case the original file is erased or rendered incorrect.

Copying Files with COPY

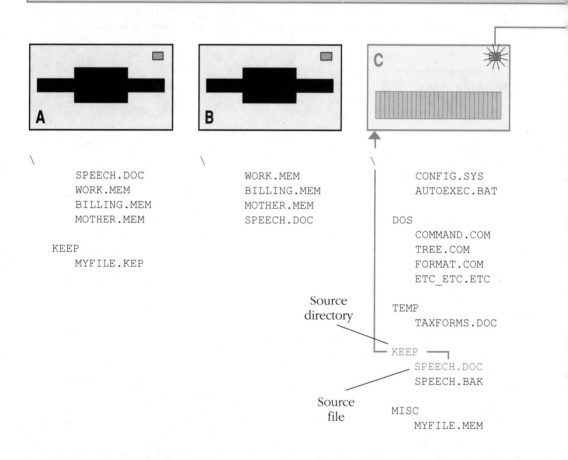

```
\                          \                          \
    SPEECH.DOC                 WORK.MEM                   CONFIG.SYS
    WORK.MEM                   BILLING.MEM                AUTOEXEC.BAT
    BILLING.MEM                MOTHER.MEM
    MOTHER.MEM                 SPEECH.DOC             DOS
                                                         COMMAND.COM
  KEEP                                                   TREE.COM
    MYFILE.KEP                                           FORMAT.COM
                                                         ETC_ETC.ETC

                                                     TEMP
                                                         TAXFORMS.DOC

                                       Source
                                     directory
                                                    KEEP
                                                         SPEECH.DOC
                                                         SPEECH.BAK

                                       Source
                                         file        MISC
                                                         MYFILE.MEM
```

In this example of COPY, a file is copied from one directory to another on the same disk. The current drive is C, and the current directory is \KEEP. Since C:\KEEP is the current drive and directory, it is omitted from the source parameters. Only the destination directory is given in the destination part of

What DOS knows by the rule of currents:
COPY C:\KEEP\SPEECH.DOC C:\MISC\SPEECH.DOC

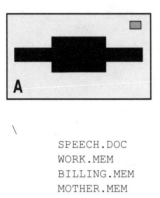

```
\
      SPEECH.DOC
      WORK.MEM
      BILLING.MEM
      MOTHER.MEM

 KEEP
      MYFILE.KEP
```

```
\
      WORK.MEM
      BILLING.MEM
      MOTHER.MEM
      SPEECH.DOC
```

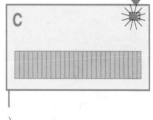

```
\
      CONFIG.SYS
      AUTOEXEC.BAT

 DOS
      COMMAND.COM
      TREE.COM
      FORMAT.COM
      ETC_ETC.ETC

 TEMP
      TAXFORMS.DOC

 KEEP
      SPEECH.DOC
      SPEECH.BAK

 MISC
      MYFILE.MEM
      SPEECH.DOC
```

Destination
directory

Destination
file

the COPY command, since C: is current and the destination file name and
extension are to match the source. DOS allows duplicate file names on the
same disk as long as they are in different directories.

Deleting and Renaming Files

When you no longer need a file, you can use the ERASE or DEL command to remove it from the disk. Erasing old work that is no longer of use is good computer housekeeping. The amount of free space on disks, especially hard disks, may get short if you do not erase old files. You can avoid this clog by erasing obsolete files.

You can use RENAME to choose a better name for a file or to make a backup file. If you use a program that overwrites a file each time the program runs, you can save the file by renaming it. You can keep both the new file and the original, renamed file.

The internal commands ERASE or DEL work exactly alike. Both commands delete files. You may find ERASE easier to remember, but DEL is quicker to type. Erasing files can be hazardous if you don't make sure you issue the command correctly. Use extreme caution when you use wild cards with the ERASE command!

The safest way to use the ERASE command is to change to the drive and directory that holds the file(s) you want to delete. You can use wild cards in the file name, but first check the file directory for other file names that match the wild card. You may not want to delete all files that match the wild card. With the current drive and directory as default type

ERASE SPEECH.DOC

or

DEL SPEECH.DOC

If you use wild cards in the command, you can erase several files at one time. DOS issues an `Are you sure?` confirmation prompt if you use the wild card ***.***. In all other cases, DOS is silent while deleting files. Caution: if you omit the file name specifier, but include a path specifier, DOS assumes that you want to use the ***.*** wild card.

DOS carries out the ERASE command when you press Enter. If you make a mistake, the Ctrl-C or Ctrl-Break key sequence may stop the ERASE command in time to minimize the damage to your files.

When you name a file, the name you choose is not permanent. You can use the RENAME (abbreviated REN) command to rename a file. The commands work exactly alike, but RENAME is probably easier to remember.

You can use RENAME to change the file name, the extension, or both. DOS assumes that a * wild card in the destination file name or extension means "use the original." Using wild cards in the source file name or extension can have unexpected results in the renaming process. Use the DIR command with the proposed wild card to see which files will be affected. Again, change to the disk and directory that contains the file(s) so that you can take advantage of DOS's defaults. You would issue a command like:

RENAME SPEECH.BAK SPEECH.DOC

Remember that you cannot duplicate a file name in the directory. If a name conflict arises, rename or erase the file with the conflicting name and then issue the RENAME command.

Deleting and Renaming Files

ERASE = DEL

Syntax for the ERASE command:

ERASE \path\filename

or

DEL \path\filename

The path is not required if the file to be erased is in the current directory. The safest way to use the ERASE command is to make the directory that holds the file to be deleted the current directory. Use the CD command for this purpose.

```
A:\>DIR

 Volume in drive A has no label
 Directory of  A:\

SPEECH   DOC      128 01-19-89   2:04p
WORK     MEM      128 01-19-89   2:31p
MOTHER   MEM      128 01-19-89   2:31p
BILLING  MEM      128 01-19-89   2:31p
         4 File(s)    353280 bytes free

A:\>ERASE WORK.MEM

A:\>DIR

 Volume in drive A has no label
 Directory of  A:\

SPEECH   DOC      128 01-19-89   2:04p
MOTHER   MEM      128 01-19-89   2:31p
BILLING  MEM      128 01-19-89   2:31p
         3 File(s)    354304 bytes free

A:\>
```

1. For added safety, issue the DIR command to see a list of files on the disk before you use ERASE.

2. Type **ERASE** and the file name.

3. To check to see that the file was erased, use the DIR command.

```
A:\>DIR

Volume in drive A has no label
Directory of  A:\

SPEECH   DOC      128 01-19-89   2:04p
WORK     MEM      128 01-19-89   2:15p
BILLING  MEM      128 01-19-89   2:16p
MOTHER   MEM      128 01-19-89   2:16p
         4 File(s)     353280 bytes free

A:\>ERASE *.MEM

A:\>DIR

Volume in drive A has no label
Directory of  A:\

SPEECH   DOC      128 01-19-89   2:04p
         1 File(s)     356352 bytes free

A:\>
```

1. Use extreme caution
   when you erase files.
   Use even more caution
   when you erase files
   using wild cards.

2. Type **ERASE *.MEM** to
   erase the files
   WORK.MEM,
   BILLING.MEM and
   MOTHER.MEM.

3. SPEECH.DOC is the only
   file shown in the
   directory listing.

```
A:\>DIR

Volume in drive A has no label
Directory of  A:\

SPEECH   DOC      128 01-19-89   2:04p
WORK     MEM      128 01-19-89   2:33p
MOTHER   MEM      128 01-19-89   2:31p
BILLING  MEM      128 01-19-89   2:31p
         4 File(s)     353280 bytes free

A:\>RENAME SPEECH.DOC SPEECH.BAK

A:\>DIR

Volume in drive A has no label
Directory of  A:\

SPEECH   BAK      128 01-19-89   2:04p
WORK     MEM      128 01-19-89   2:33p
MOTHER   MEM      128 01-19-89   2:31p
BILLING  MEM      128 01-19-89   2:31p
         4 File(s)     353280 bytes free

A:\>
```

1. Renaming files is another
   valuable disk-
   maintenance command.

2. The directory listing
   shows that the file
   SPEECH.DOC is now
   named SPEECH.BAK.

8

Protecting Data

In this chapter you will learn how to

• Prevent hardware failure

• Prevent software failure

• Use the BACKUP command

• Use the RESTORE command

As you use your computer, you will create a multitude of files. Many of these files will contain information you find very important. With the reliability of today's computers, it is tempting to think of your files as being "there when you need them." But as the old computer saying goes, "There are two kinds of computer users—those who have lost precious files and those who are going to." This chapter describes how to protect files from a variety of menaces, such as static electricity, excessive heat, and erratic electrical power.

The most important protection you can have is learning to make backup copies of your disk files. Although DISKCOPY and COPY are adequate for making "safety" copies of floppy disks, hard disk files are often too big to fit on a floppy disk. And yet, just one errant wild card ERASE command can delete dozens of files from a hard disk in seconds. What can you do for insurance against the loss of hours of work? You can use the DOS BACKUP command to make regular backup disks of your files. Of course, you also should know how to use the complement to BACKUP, the RESTORE

Introduction   Avoiding   Preparing for   Issuing the BACKUP
                Data Loss   the Backup   and RESTORE
                                                Commands

command. RESTORE takes your backup disks and places these files on your hard disk.

In this chapter, you will learn the basics of the BACKUP and RESTORE commands. Using the examples in this chapter, you will learn to back up and restore your entire hard disk. You also will learn the various switches to use to adapt the BACKUP and RESTORE commands. The BACKUP and RESTORE commands are effective insurance against the loss of precious files.

If you have never learned how to back up your disk files, now is the time to learn! If you are just learning your way around DOS, this chapter is a must. Apply this chapter's information, and you may never again experience the sinking feeling that comes to those who lose files.

Key Terms Used in This Chapter

Surge suppresser   A protective device inserted between a power outlet and a computer's power plug. Surge suppressers help block power surges that could damage the computer's circuits.

Static electricity   A charge that builds on an object and that can be discharged when another object is touched. Electronic circuits can be damaged by static electricity discharges.

Ground   An electrical path directly to the center prong of an outlet. Grounds can safely dissipate static discharges.

Voltage regulator   An electrical device that keeps voltage fluctuations from reaching an electrical device. Regulators usually don't stop power surges.

Avoiding Data Loss

Today's personal computers are reliable and economical data processing machines. The PCs of today do the work of computers that a decade ago only a few fortunate users had access to. Like any machine, however, computers are subject to failures and operator errors.

Preventing Hardware Failures

Computers contain thousands of transistorized circuits. Most of these circuits have life expectancies of more than a century. However, a poor power source, excessive heat, and static discharges can cause circuits to fail or operate erratically. Disk drives have precise moving parts with critical alignments. The potential always exists for hardware failures. If you follow the precautions presented in this section, you reduce the likelihood of hardware failure.

Always be cautious about your computer's environment. If your power flutters and lights flicker, you might need to purchase a line voltage regulator from your computer dealer. Make sure that any electrical appliances you have near your computer do not pollute your power source.

Is the fan on the back of your computer choked with dust? Clean the air vents and check that your computer has room to breathe. Your computer can do unexpected things when it is too hot. Because circuits are not reliable when they overheat, you may get jumbled data. The moral is: make sure that your computer can breathe and keep it cool.

You generate *static electricity* on your body when humidity is low, you wear synthetic fabrics, or you walk on carpet. Just by touching your keyboard while carrying a static charge, you can send an electrical shudder through your computer. This can cause data jumble or circuit failure. Fortunately, you can avoid static problems by touching your grounded system cabinet before touching the keyboard. If static electricity is a serious problem for you, ask your dealer about anti-static products.

Preventing Software Failures

Each software program you buy is a set of instructions for the microprocessor. A small minority of software packages have flawed instructions called *bugs*. Software bugs are usually minor and rarely cause more than keyboard lock-ups or jumbled displays. The potential does exist for a software bug to cause your disk drive to operate in an erratic way, however. Fortunately, most companies test and debug their software before marketing the packages. Performing a backup of your disks is your best insurance against bugs.

Preventing Your Mistakes

As you gain skill, you will use DOS commands that can result in the unplanned loss of files. Commands such as COPY, ERASE, and FORMAT carry out their jobs as you command them. DOS has no way of knowing when a correct command line will have an unintended effect. For this reason, make a mental note to study what you type before you press Enter. It is easy to develop a typing rhythm that carries you straight through confirmation prompts into the clutches of disaster. Remember that you can use Ctrl-C, Ctrl-Break and, if necessary, Ctrl-Alt-Del to abandon commands. Because you are sure to make mistakes, always have a backup copy of your files.

Avoiding Data Loss

Power strips keep your cables neat and get rid of standard extension cords. Many power strips have power surge suppressers built-in.

Line voltage regulators remove dips in power lines caused either by motors turning on or by other power reducers.

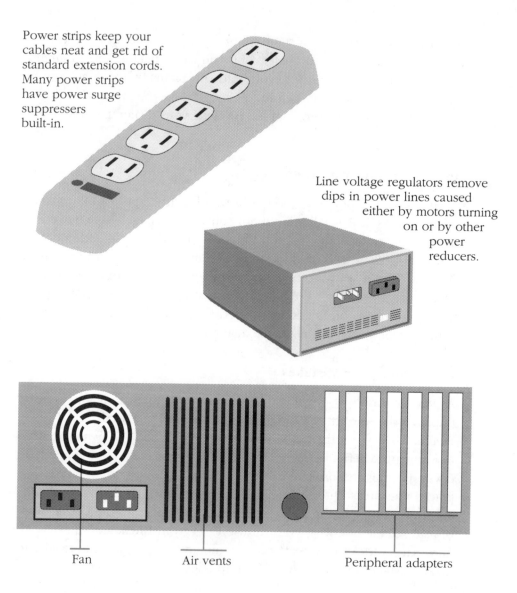

Fan   Air vents   Peripheral adapters

Use a soft blind-cleaner attachment on your vacuum cleaner to occasionally remove dust build-up from your computer's "breathing" system.

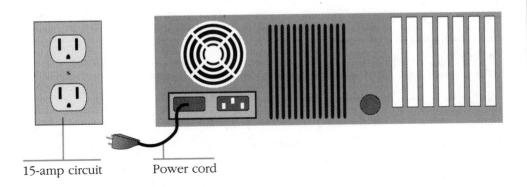

15-amp circuit   Power cord

Try to connect your computer equipment to a power source that isn't shared by copiers, TVs, fans, or other "noise" generating electrical equipment.

Hardware and Software Problems and Remedies

Problem	Remedy
Static electricity	Anti-static liquid Anti-static floor mat "Touch Pad" on desk
Overheating	Clean clogged air vents Remove objects blocking vents Use air-conditioned room in summer
Damaged disks	Don't leave disks to be warped by sun Use protective covers Avoid spilling liquids on disks Store disks in a safe place Avoid magnetic fields from appliances (TVs, microwave ovens, etc.)
Software bugs	Buy tested commercial products

Preparing for the Backup

The BACKUP command selectively copies files from your hard disk to the destination floppy disk. The internal format of the backed up file on the floppy is different from normal files. Therefore, you cannot use COPY to retrieve files stored on a backup disk. The RESTORE command takes the files from your backup disks and copies them on your hard disk.

Your computer may have a tape backup unit as part of its peripheral hardware. The methods used for backing up files to tape vary. You should know how to do disk-based backups, however, in case you need to restore files to a computer that is not equipped with a tape backup.

You can use the BACKUP command to back up an entire fixed disk with one command. You also can use switches and parameters to make partial backups of the disk, backing up selected files only. You can select files by time, date, directory, activity, and by file name.

Full Backup Considerations

A full backup makes backup copies of all files on the hard disk. BACKUP even copies hidden files. When you perform a full backup, you have the complete contents of your fixed disk on backup floppy disks.

How Often To Back Up

Doing a complete backup about once a month is a good work habit. If you do not plan to do partial backups that copy important files, then do a complete backup more often. On any day, ask yourself, "If my hard drive failed today, how much data would I lose?" It is much easier to perform a backup than to try to reconstruct lost data. DOS does not prompt you to make backups. The decision is yours. Let your conscience be your guide. Remember, it's your data.

Introduction   Avoiding   **Preparing for**   Issuing the BACKUP
                     Data Loss   **the Backup**   and RESTORE
                                                         Commands

Preparing Backup Floppies

Before you do a complete backup, make sure that you have enough
floppy disks to hold all the files. You don't want to run out to the
computer store in the middle of a backup to buy more disks!

DOS versions 3.3 and 4.0 are more efficient than older versions in
utilizing backup space. You can use some rules of thumb when you
calculate the space you need for an entire backup.

To get an idea of how full your hard disk is, change to drive C. Type
**C:CD **. You can then issue the DIR command. Take the number of
free bytes the directory displays and divide the number by 1,000,000.
The remainder gives you a ballpark figure of the number of megabytes
left on the disk. Subtract the number of megabytes from the disk's total
capacity. You now have the approximate number of megabytes that
you need to perform the backup. When you know the approximate
number of megabytes, you can use Table 8.1 to estimate the number
of disks you will need. If you run out of disks, you can stop the
backup by pressing Ctrl-C. The worst consequence is your lost time.

Format the disks and number them consecutively. BACKUP copies
disks in order so that RESTORE can place the files on your hard disk in
the proper order. Do not use the /S switch when you format the disks.
The /S switch decreases the available space on floppy disks. You can
use any disks that contain files you no longer want to keep. BACKUP
overwrites old files. When you finish the backup, arrange the disks
numerically. Place them in a convenient part of your work space
where they will stay in sequence.

If you have DOS V3.3, you can skip the formatting step. Simply
include a /F (format) switch when you issue the BACKUP command.
DOS V4.0 detects unformatted disks and formats them. Note that the
BACKUP command itself will take longer to execute when BACKUP
takes care of the formatting for you.

Preparing for the Backup

JANUARY						
1	2	3	4	5	6	7
8	9	10	11	12	13	14
15	16	BACK UP	18	19	20	21
22	23	24	25	26	27	28
29	30	31				

Try to pick a time at some regular interval to do a backup. Backup once per month—more often if you frequently change many files.

Get into the habit of performing a backup at least once a month. Mark the date on the calendar so you do not forget.

Follow these steps to back up your hard disk:

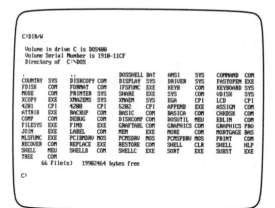

```
C>DIR/W

Volume in drive C is DOS400
Volume Serial Number is 1910-11CF
Directory of  C:\DOS

.            ..            DOSSHELL BAT   ANSI     SYS   COMMAND  COM
COUNTRY  SYS   DISKCOPY COM   DISPLAY  SYS   DRIVER   SYS   FASTOPEN EXE
FDISK    COM   FORMAT   COM   IFSFUNC  EXE   KEYB     COM   KEYBOARD SYS
MODE     COM   PRINTER  SYS   SHARE    EXE   SYS      COM   VDISK    SYS
XCOPY    EXE   XMA2EMS  SYS   XMAEM    SYS   EGA      CPI   LCD      CPI
4201     CPI   4208     CPI   5202     CPI   APPEND   EXE   ASSIGN   COM
ATTRIB   EXE   BACKUP   COM   BASIC    COM   BASICA   COM   CHKDSK   COM
COMP     COM   DEBUG    COM   DISKCOMP COM   DOSUTIL  MEU   EDLIN    COM
FILESYS  EXE   FIND     EXE   GRAFTABL COM   GRAPHICS COM   GRAPHICS PRO
JOIN     EXE   LABEL    COM   MEM      EXE   MORE     COM   MORTGAGE BAS
NLSFUNC  EXE   PCIBMDRV MOS   PCMSDRV  MOS   PCMSPDRV MOS   PRINT    COM
RECOVER  COM   REPLACE  EXE   RESTORE  COM   SHELL    CLR   SHELL    HLP
SHELL    MEU   SHELLB   COM   SHELLC   EXE   SORT     EXE   SUBST    EXE
TREE     COM
      66 File(s)   19902464 bytes free

C>
```

Estimate how full your hard disk is.

Calculate the number of floppy disks needed (see table 8.1):

Capacity in megabytes of disk
— Megabytes left
_____

Megabytes used

Format the floppies or use BACKUP /F if you have DOS V3.3.

Table 8.1
Determining the Number of Floppy Disks Needed for a Backup.

Megabytes Used	Disk Capacity			
	360K	*720K*	*1.2M*	*1.44M*
10M	29	15	9	8
20M	59	29	18	15
30M	83	44	27	22
40M	116	58	35	29
70M	200	100	60	50

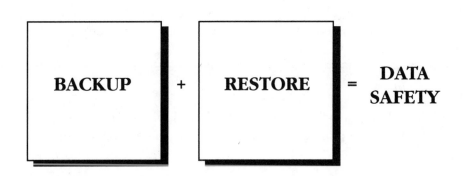

BACKUP + **RESTORE** = **DATA SAFETY**

(BACKUP is, in effect, just half a command. You need the other half, RESTORE, to retrieve files copied with BACKUP.)

Issuing the BACKUP and RESTORE Commands

Syntax for BACKUP

Your computer can use the files produced by BACKUP only after you run them through the RESTORE program. BACKUP is an external command; therefore you should include its path in the command line. Or the command file should be in the directory where the BACKUP command resides. The symbolic syntax for BACKUP is

BACKUP *sd:spath\sfilename.ext dd: /switches*

The *sd:* is the letter of the drive that contains the source disk. This drive is usually the C drive. The *spath* symbolizes the path to the files you want to make backups of. The *sfilename.ext* notation is the full file name of the file(s) you want to back up. Full file names may contain wild cards for selective backup of matching files. The *dd:* is the drive that receives the backup files. The */switches* are optional switches that modify the basic BACKUP command. Not all switches are available on all versions of DOS. The DOS defaults also may vary from version to version. You can use the examples in this chapter as a model for your commands.

Full Backup

The full backup puts all files on your backup floppies. The full backup requires about one minute for each floppy disk to be used in the backup.

Change to the root directory and enter the command

BACKUP C:*.* A:/S

This command tells DOS to back up all files from the root directory and to include all subdirectories (/S switch) in the directory tree to drive A. DOS prompts you when to insert and change disks. Always put the backup date on the disks for future reference. Put the backup disks in the proper sequence and store the disks in a safe place.

Introduction
Avoiding
Data Loss
Preparing for
the Backup
**Issuing the BACKUP
and RESTORE
Commands**

Selective Backups

By specifying source directory paths, wild card file names or
extensions, and switches, you can select specific files to back up.
Selective backups are useful when only some of your data changes
between full backups or when you want to move specific files from
one computer system to another.

Specifying Selected Directory and File Names

BACKUP always starts in the directory you place in the path. If you
place a directory name in the path that is at some point in the tree
other than root, you can back up files in that directory (and its
directories with /S). You can add further selectivity by using wild cards
in the file name. For example, placing *.DOC in the file name would
give you a backup of files with the extension DOC.

Adding Other Switches

The /M switch selects only the files that have changed since the last
backup. The /D and /T switches select files based on date and, in
versions 3.3 and 4.0, on the time. Use the /D and /T switches when
you want to select files based on a date or specific time. You enter a
date and, optionally, a time after the appropriate switch, using the
same formats you use for the DATE and TIME commands.

Files changed on or after a specified date and time will be included in
the backup. The /A switch adds files to a backup disk series and
leaves the existing backup files intact. The /F switch formats the
destination floppy as part of the BACKUP procedure in DOS V3.3. If
needed, DOS V4.0 automatically formats the floppy if necessary.

The FORMAT command must also be accessible in the current path.
You first select the files with the directory path and then use the
switches to apply further selectivity. Consult the graphics spread for
examples.

Issuing the BACKUP and RESTORE Commands

Syntax for RESTORE

The partner command to BACKUP is the DOS external command, RESTORE. RESTORE is the only command that copies backed-up files to the hard disk. RESTORE's syntax is very similar to BACKUP's syntax. Seen symbolically, the syntax is

RESTORE *sd: dd:\dpath\dfilename.ext /switches*

sd: is the source disk letter that holds the floppies you want to restore. The *dd:* is the hard disk that you want to restore to (usually the C drive). The *dpath* is the directory on the hard disk which will receive the restored files. Files on the backup floppies that didn't come from the *dpath* will not be restored. The *dfilename.ext* is the file name for the file(s) to be restored. You can use wild cards in the file name to select specific files. */switches* stands for the optional switches you can add to gain further selectivity to the RESTORE command.

Restoring One File

You can choose to restore a single file by using a complete path and file name in the command. As in all selective restores, DOS prompts you to insert sequential disks until it locates the specified file. Suppose that you want to restore the file \KEEP\SPEECH.DOC from the backup disk. The proper syntax is

RESTORE A: C:\KEEP\SPEECH.DOC

Restoring More than One File

You can choose to restore more than one file. For example, suppose that you want to restore all files with a TXT extension to the \KEEP directory. The command to type is

RESTORE A: C:\KEEP*.TXT

The wild card *.TXT selects all files with the TXT extension from the KEEP directory.

If you want to restore all files in a directory *and* all subdirectories below the directory, use the **/S** switch. The command **RESTORE A: C:\KEEP*.* /S** would restore all files in directories subordinate to \KEEP directory. For example, the file MOMS.LET in the subdirectory LETTERS would restore to the KEEP directory.

Avoiding DOS Version Conflicts

Starting with version 3.3, DOS uses a different method to produce the contents of a backup disk. DOS versions 3.3 and greater can restore files that you backed up with previous versions of DOS. Versions earlier than 3.3, however, cannot restore backups made with versions 3.3 or 4.0. Although you cannot take files backed up with newer versions of DOS and restore them on computers with earlier versions of DOS, you can use COPY to move the files. Also realize that if you restore all files from a full backup to a computer with a different version of DOS, the hidden system files and utility command programs will be those taken from the backup files. Finally, the restore program from another MS-DOS vendor may simply not work.

Issuing the BACKUP and RESTORE Commands

BACKUP C:*.* A:/S

```
\
|   CONFIG.SYS
|   AUTOEXEC.BAT
|   (Hidden files)
|—— DOS
|       COMMAND.COM
|       TREE.COM
|       FORMAT.COM
|       ETC_ETC.ETC.
|—— TEMP
|       TAXFORMS.DOC
|—— KEEP
|   |   MYFILE.TXT
|   |   SALESREP.TXT
|   |   SPEECH.DOC
|   |   SPEECH.BAK
|   |—— LETTERS
|               MOMS.LET
|—— MISC
        MYFILE.MEM
        SPEECH.DOC
```

Backup all files on C

BACKUP C:\KEEP*.* A:/S

```
\
    CONFIG.SYS
    AUTOEXEC.BAT
    (Hidden files)
—— DOS
        COMMAND.COM
        TREE.COM
        FORMAT.COM
        ETC_ETC.ETC.
—— TEMP
        TAXFORMS.DOC
—— KEEP
    |   MYFILE.TXT
    |   SALESREP.TXT
    |   SPEECH.DOC
    |   SPEECH.BAK
    |—— LETTERS
                MOMS.LET
—— MISC
        MYFILE.MEM
        SPEECH.DOC
```

Backup all files in \KEEP and its subordinate subdirectories. (In this case \KEEP\LETTERS.)

BACKUP C:*.DOC A:/S

```
\
    CONFIG.SYS
    AUTOEXEC.BAT
    (Hidden files)
—— DOS
        COMMAND.COM
        TREE.COM
        FORMAT.COM
        ETC_ETC.ETC.
—— TEMP
        TAXFORMS.DOC
—— KEEP
    |   MYFILE.TXT
    |   SALESREP.TXT
    |   SPEECH.DOC
    |   SPEECH.BAK
    |—— LETTERS
                MOMS.LET
—— MISC
        MYFILE.MEM
        SPEECH.DOC
```

Backup all files on drive C: with DOC extensions.

BACKUP C:\DOS A:

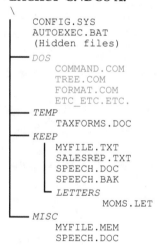

```
\
    CONFIG.SYS
    AUTOEXEC.BAT
    (Hidden files)
—— DOS
        COMMAND.COM
        TREE.COM
        FORMAT.COM
        ETC_ETC.ETC.
—— TEMP
        TAXFORMS.DOC
—— KEEP
    |   MYFILE.TXT
    |   SALESREP.TXT
    |   SPEECH.DOC
    |   SPEECH.BAK
    |—— LETTERS
                MOMS.LET
—— MISC
        MYFILE.MEM
        SPEECH.DOC
```

Backup all files in the DOS directory only.

(RESTORE in these cases acts on the same files.)

186

Introduction

Avoiding
Data Loss

Preparing for
the Backup

**Issuing the BACKUP
and RESTORE
Commands**

Table 8.2
BACKUP and RESTORE Switches

BACKUP

/M	Selects files whose contents have changed since the last BACKUP command backed them up.
/D	Selects files based on the date.
/T	Selects files based on the time (V3.3 and 4.0).
/A	Adds files to an existing backup disk series and leaves the existing backup files intact.
/F	Formats the destination floppy as part of the BACKUP procedure in V3.3. V4.0 automatically formats the floppy if needed.

RESTORE

/P	Prompts the user if the file should be restored if it has been marked as read only or has been changed since the last backup.
/N	Only files that are no longer on the hard disk. This switch is useful if hard disk files were deleted accidentally and need restored from backups. (new in DOS 3.3)
/M	Does the same as /N but also restores files that have changed since the backup. (new in DOS 3.3)
/B:date	Restores all files created or modified on or *before* the date.
/A:date	Restores all files created or modified on or *after* the specified date. This switch uses the DATE command format.
/E:time	Restores all files modified at or *earlier* than the specified time. This switch uses the TIME command format.
/L:time	Restores all files modified at or *later* than the specified time.

9

Special
Commands

In this chapter you will learn how to

- Redirect the input and output of DOS commands

- Create text files using the CON device

- Use the CHKDSK command

- Obtain from DOS a report on available memory

Although DOS has dozens of commands, some are not as useful as others. Some long-time DOS users have not used half of the available DOS commands. This chapter looks at some of the more common DOS commands that you will find useful in your computing. You can think of these as DOS "survival" commands.

You will find that with just a few DOS commands, you can do the majority of your work.

This chapter also covers the topics of DOS devices and redirection. The section on redirection will teach you how to change both the standard source and standard destination of input and output.

188

Key Terms Used in This Chapter

Redirection	Taking input from some place other than the keyboard or sending output to some place other than the screen.
Device	A hardware component or peripheral that DOS can use in some commands as though it were a file.
Console	The device DOS uses for keyboard input and screen output. DOS recognizes the console as CON.
ASCII file	A file whose contents are alphanumeric and control characters, which can be text or other information readable by humans.
Pipe	A method of taking the output of one command and making it the input for another command in DOS.
Filter	A method of selecting certain outputs from complete inputs.

DOS Devices and Redirection

In DOS, the term *redirection* means to change the source or destination normally used for input and output. The standard input device is the keyboard. The standard output device is the screen display. When you use the keyboard to type a command, COMMAND.COM carries the text or messages and displays them on-screen. In DOS, the keyboard and display are the standard, or default, *devices* for messages, prompts, and input.

DOS Devices

DOS views devices as extensions of the main unit of the computer. Examples of devices are the keyboard, the video display, and the printer. DOS controls devices through its system files and the ROM BIOS. Fortunately, the details of how DOS handles the devices are not important. Devices can be classified as input, output, or input and output. For example, a disk can be an input or an output device. The keyboard is an input device, but the display is an output device. The serial adapter and printer adapter can send output and receive input.

You can use device names, just like file names, in some commands. In fact, DOS treats devices as if they were files. Device names are three to four characters long and do not contain extensions. You cannot delete device names or format them, but you can use device names in commands to do some very handy things.

The COPY CON Device

As a useful example of using a DOS device, you can create a file that contains characters you input directly from the keyboard. You'll use the familiar COPY command. This time, however, you will copy data from the CON or *console device*. CON is DOS's device name for the keyboard. You can send the characters to a file named TEST.TXT. At the DOS prompt type

COPY CON TEST.TXT

You have just told DOS: "Copy data from the console and send the output to the file TEST.TXT."

When you press Enter, the cursor drops to the next line and no DOS prompt appears. You can begin typing characters as the input to the file. Each time you press Enter, DOS holds the line you typed in RAM. You can type several lines, and when you finish, press F6 or Ctrl-Z. DOS recognizes F6 or Ctrl-Z as the end-of-file character. After you press F6 or Ctrl-Z, the information you typed is entered into the new file and DOS displays on-screen the `1 file(s) copied` message. To verify that the new file exists, you can perform a DIR and look for the file name TEST.TXT. You have just entered a text file into your computer using a DOS device!

Redirection Symbols

You must use special redirection symbols to tell DOS to use non-default devices in a command. The redirection symbols are <, >, and >>. The < symbol points away from the device or file and says, "Take input from here." The > symbol points toward the device or file and says, "Put output there." The >> symbol redirects a program's output, but adds the text to an established file. When you issue a redirection command, place the redirection symbol after the DOS command but before the device name.

DOS Devices and Redirection

Displaying a Text File with TYPE

To display the contents of the new text file, use the DOS TYPE command. TYPE tells DOS to send the contents of a file to the display. At the DOS prompt type

TYPE TEST.TXT

DOS takes input from the TEST.TXT file up to the end-of-file marker and displays it on your screen. The TYPE command works on text files, which are called ASCII files. Don't bother trying to use the TYPE command to display files with the extensions COM and EXE. Both of these extensions are for program files and indicate binary files. The extensions MOS and OVL also indicate binary files.

Redirecting to a Printer

Wouldn't it be great to get the output of a DIR or TREE command on your printer? You can, by redirecting output to the DOS device PRN (the printer). Make sure that you have the printer turned on and connected to your computer. Now type

DIR/W >PRN

When you press Enter, the output of the DIR command goes to the printer. The /W (wide display) switch puts the files in five columns. You can tuck the output into the sleeve of a floppy disk to identify the contents of a disk.

Introduction

DOS Devices
and
Redirection

Other Useful
Commands

If you entered text into the TEST.TXT file and your printer is ready, type the command

TYPE TEST.TXT >PRN

You now have a printed copy of the TEST.TXT file.

Never try to redirect binary files to the printer. Redirecting binary data can result in paper feed problems, beeps, meaningless graphics characters, and maybe a locked computer. If you get "hung," you can do a warm boot or turn the power switch off and then on again.

Pipes and Filters

The output of one command can be presented as the input of the commands FIND, SORT, and MORE. The symbol that presents or *pipes* output from one of these three commands, or *filters*, is the | symbol. A *filter* is a program that gets data from the standard input, modifies the data, and then writes the modified data to the display.

FIND, SORT, and MORE accept the output of a DOS command and do additional processing on that output. SORT alphabetizes output. FIND outputs lines that match characters given on the command line. MORE displays a prompt when each screen of the output is full.

DOS Devices and Redirection

Some devices send input and receive output and some do both.
Other devices can be used for input only (the keyboard) or output
only (the video display or printer).

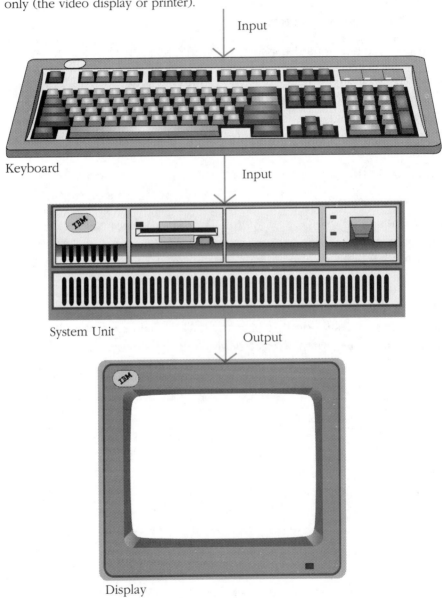

Input

Keyboard   Input

System Unit   Output

Display

The standards for input and output. The
keyboard is used for input, and the video
display for output of prompts and messages.

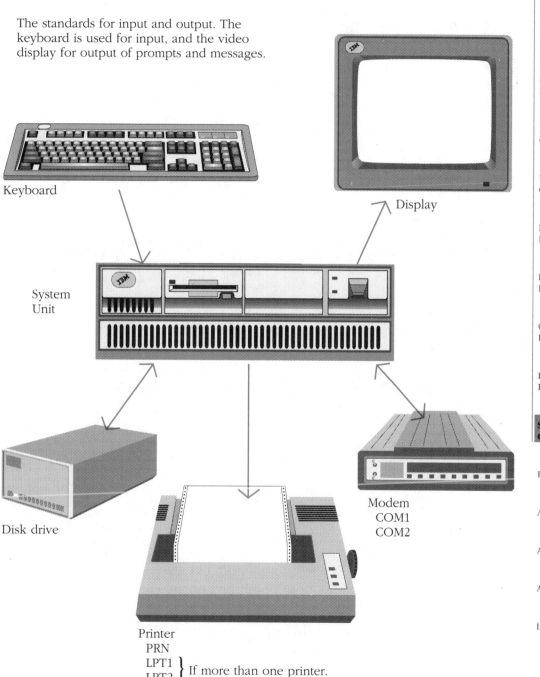

Keyboard

Display

System
Unit

Disk drive

Modem
COM1
COM2

Printer
PRN
LPT1
LPT2 } If more than one printer.

195

DOS Devices and Redirection

Using COPY CON

```
A>COPY CON TEST.TXT
```

When you type this line and press Enter, the cursor moves to the beginning of the next line.

```
A>COPY CON TEST.TXT

This is a file copied
quickly between a disk and a
device.
```

Type the following line: **This is a file copied quickly between a disk and a device.** Press Enter and then press F6.

```
A>COPY CON TEST.TXT

This is a file copied
quickly between a disk and a
device.

^Z

1File(s) copied
```

DOS reports how many files you successfully copied.

```
TYPE TEST.TXT

This is a file copied
quickly between a disk and a
device.
```

You can display the contents of the TEST.TXT file by typing **TYPE TEST.TXT** and pressing Enter.

Table 9.1
DOS Device Names

Name	Device
CON	The video display and keyboard.
AUX or COM1	The first asynchronous communications port. If a second asynchronous port is available, it is called COM2.
LPT1 or PRN	The first line or parallel printer. This device is used only for output.
LPT2	The second parallel printer.
LPT3	The third parallel printer.
NUL	A dummy device (for redirecting output to "nowhere.")

Table 9.2
The Symbols for Redirection

<	Redirects a program's input
>	Redirects a program's output
>>	Redirects a program's output but adds the text to an established file.

DOS Devices and Redirection

TYPE and MORE

```
C>TYPE TEST.TXT

This is a file created
by a device and displayed
by the TYPE command. This
is a file created by a
device and displayed by
the TYPE command. This is
a file created by a device
and displayed by the TYPE
command.
```

The TYPE command displays the contents of a text file. To use TYPE, you must enter the command and the full name of the file. Wild cards are not allowed. The TYPE command sends the contents of the file to the standard output, that is the CONsole, or screen.

```
C>TYPE TEST.TXT > PRN
```

To get a printed copy of the TEST.TXT file, type **TEST.TXT > PRN**.

```
C>TYPE TEST.TXT

This is a file created
by a device and displayed
by the TYPE command. This
is a file created by a
device and displayed by
the TYPE command. This is
```

To pause the display, use the Ctrl-S, Ctrl-Num Lock, or Pause keys. Press any key to resume the display.

```
C>TYPE TEST.TXT | MORE

This is a file created
by a device and displayed
by the TYPE command. This
is a file created by a
device and displayed by
the TYPE command. This is

--More--
```

The MORE filter displays one screen of information and pauses while displaying the message —More—. When you press any key, MORE displays the next screen of text.

Introduction

DOS Devices
and
Redirection

Other Useful
Commands

FIND and SORT

```
C>DIR | FIND "<DIR>"

DOS  <DIR>  12-27-88   12:30p
TEMP <DIR>  12-27-88   12:37p
KEEP <DIR>  12-28-88    9:12a
MISC <DIR>  12-29-88   11:59p
```

You can use the FIND command to filter the output of a DIR command. FIND will display on the screen only the lines that contain <DIR>. The | symbol pipes the output of DIR to FIND.

The SORT command is a filter that alphabetizes its input. In this example, the output of the DIR command is piped to SORT. When the directory is displayed on the screen, it is in alphabetical order.

```
C>DIR | SORT

 6 File(s)   12595200 bytes free
Directory of C:\
Volume in drive C is 10_MEG
AUTOEXEC  BAT  12-27-88    9:20a
CONFIG    SYS  12-30-88   10:01a
DOS       <DIR> 12-27-88   12:30p
KEEP      <DIR> 12-28-88    1:22p
MISC      <DIR> 12-29-88   11:59p
TEMP      <DIR> 12-27-88   12:37p
C>
```

Other Useful Commands

The commands presented so far should enable you to get control over your computer. This section offers additional commands that you will find useful.

CLS (Clear Screen)

The internal CLS command erases or clears the display and positions the cursor at the top left corner of the blank screen. Use CLS when the screen becomes too "busy" with the contents of previous commands' output. CLS has no parameters. You simply enter CLS at the DOS prompt, and the screen clears.

MEM (Memory Report)

The MEM command is new in DOS 4.0. MEM causes DOS to report the amount of system memory available for programs to load and run. In its simple form, you can issue MEM from the DOS prompt with no parameters. You can redirect MEM's output to the PRN device.

VER (DOS Version)

The VER command indicates the DOS version your computer is using. VER is useful if you must work on another person's computer. You can issue this command before you start work to see which DOS version you will be working with. In this way, you know which commands or switches the computer accepts. VER is also useful when you boot your system from a disk you did not prepare. The floppy may contain system files from a version of DOS you normally do not use. The VER command has no parameters and is issued at the DOS prompt.

VERIFY (File Writing Verification)

VERIFY is the command you use to check the accuracy of data written to disks. Verify has one parameter which is ON or OFF. When you type **VERIFY ON** at the prompt, DOS re-reads all data to insure that it was written correctly. VERIFY ON causes DOS to operate a bit slower; therefore you might want to use the command only with important data. Type **VERIFY OFF** to turn verification off again. To display the current status of verify as being either on or off, type **VERIFY**.

VOL (Display Volume Name)

You recall that the /V switch used with the **FORMAT** command enables you to enter a disk volume name for a disk you are formatting. When you type **VOL** at the DOS prompt, DOS displays the volume name of the current disk. Viewing volume names is much easier than wading through directory listings when you sort through floppies.

CHKDSK (Check Disk)

CHKDSK is an external command that checks disk space and reports disk and memory status. CHKDSK can also repair certain errors on the disk. Because CHKDSK is an external command, you must specify a path to its directory with the PATH command or give the path on the command line. The symbolic syntax for CHKDSK is

CHKDSK *d:path\filename.ext* /F/V

Other Useful Commands

The *d:* is the name of the drive that contains the disk you want to check. *path* is the directory and *filename.ext* is the file name. The /F switch tells DOS to fix problems on the disk if errors are found. The /V switch is the verbose switch. The /V switch causes DOS to display detailed information about any errors detected.

You can use wild cards in the file specifier. By the rule of currents, you can omit the names of the current disk and directory, and the command will use the DOS defaults. You can redirect the output of CHKDSK to the printer if you do not use the /F switch.

CHKDSK /F

In this instance, the /F switch causes DOS to ask you before it fixes problems the command has detected. Avoid using /F until you know the implications of the fix action. The *MS-DOS User's Guide,* 3rd Edition, explains the /F actions in detail and should be consulted if CHKDSK finds problems.

CHKDSK before a Backup

One of the more useful features of CHKDSK is its ability to report the number of bytes used in directories, user files, and hidden files. You can use CHKDSK before you issue the BACKUP command to determine the number of bytes to be backed up. Divide the number of bytes by the capacity of your backup floppies. Space on floppies is usually measured in kilobytes or megabytes. Divide the number of bytes to be backed up by 1000 for kilobytes or 1,000,000 for megabytes. You then can approximate the number of floppies you will need to do the backup.

For example, suppose that you want to back up a hard disk but don't know how many floppies to prepare. You can issue the command **CHKDSK C:** and DOS will check the directory on your logged disk and issue a report. The report gives you the disk's total capacity in bytes, the number of hidden files and their byte total, the number of directories and their byte total, and the number of user files and their byte total. The report also gives the total memory bytes in RAM and the number of RAM bytes that are free for use.

If you add the number of bytes in hidden files, directories, and user files, you have the number of bytes to be backed up. Normally the hidden files and directory files do not add up to more than 100K. You will be safe using the user files total to calculate the number of floppies you need for a backup.

CHKDSK and Fragmentation

One of the messages given by CHKDSK concerns non-contiguous blocks in files. This condition is known as *fragmentation*. It means that as you delete and add files, gaps occur. Each new file cannot be stored in a single space on the disk. Fragmentation is not serious. It happens to all active disks. At worse, fragmentation slows down disk operations slightly. Chapter 7 shows you how to help fragmented disks.

Other Useful Commands

MEM

```
655360 bytes total memory

655360 bytes available

572944 largest executable
program size
```

The DOS 4.0 MEM command reports the amount of system memory available for programs to load and run.

VER

```
C>VER

IBM Personal Computer DOS
Version 3.30
```

The VER command indicates which version of DOS your computer is using.

VERIFY

```
C>VERIFY

VERIFY is off
```

VERIFY checks the accuracy of data written to disks. Type VERIFY and press Enter. DOS displays the current status of VERIFY.

VOL

```
C>VOL a:

Volume in drive A has no
label.
```

The VOL command displays the volume name of a disk if you entered one when you formatted the disk.

CHKDSK

```
C>CHKDSK
Volume Serial Number is 146E-3CA4
30203904 bytes total disk space
71680 bytes in 2 hidden files
114688 bytes in 48 directories
26601472 bytes in 1334 user files
30720 bytes in bad sectors
3385344 bytes available on disk

2048 bytes in each allocation unit
14748 total allocation units on disk
1653 available allocation units on disk

655360 total bytes memory
234144 bytes free
```

CHKDSK provides a detailed report of disk and memory status.

```
FILE0000 CHK    FILE0001 CHK    FILE0002 CHK
FILE0005 CHK    FILE0006 CHK    FILE0007 CHK
FILE0010 CHK    FILE0011 CHK    FILE0012 CHK
FILE0015 CHK    FILE0016 CHK    FILE0017 CHK
FILE0020 CHK    FILE0021 CHK
        22 File(s)     366592 bytes free

A:\>
```

The CHKDSK/F command causes DOS to ask you if it should fix problems the command has detected. A common "fix" is to convert lost clusters into files, which you can delete if they are not useful. CHKDSK assigns these files names as shown on-screen. Files that are no longer useful may be safely deleted.

```
C>CHKDSK COMMAND.COM
Volume Serial Number is 146E-3CA4
30203904 bytes total disk space
71680 bytes in 2 hidden files
114688 bytes in 48 directories
26605568 bytes in 1336 user files
30720 bytes in bad sectors
3381248 bytes available on disk

2048 bytes in each allocation unit
14748 total allocation units on disk
1651 available allocation units on disk

655360 total bytes memory
234144 bytes free

C:\COMMAND.COM Contains 2 non-
contiguous blocks
```

CHKDSK will report whether a file is fragmented, that is not stored in contiguous blocks. In this example, COMMAND.COM is the file on which CHKDSK reports.

```
C>CHKDSK > PRN
```

Redirecting CHKDSK's output to the printer is a practical way to preserve the information generated by the command.

10

Batch Files

In this chapter you will learn

- How to create the text for a batch file

- About the AUTOEXEC.BAT and CONFIG.SYS files

- About some useful sample batch files

A *batch file* is a text file that contains DOS commands. DOS executes the commands in the batch file one line at a time, treating them as though you had issued each one individually.

Batch files always have the extension BAT in their full file names. When you type a batch file's name at the DOS prompt, COMMAND.COM looks in the current directory for that file name with the BAT extension, reads the file, and executes the DOS commands the file contains. The whole process is automatic. You enter the batch file name and DOS does the work.

Batch files are useful for automatically issuing commands that are hard to remember or that are easy to mistype at the command line. A good example would be some form of the BACKUP command. BACKUP is not a difficult command, but it is a command that you will use far less frequently than you use the COPY command or the DIR command. You may find it convenient to put properly formed backup commands in batch files that you can execute with one simple batch name. This chapter contains a batch file for a full system backup that you can use as presented or change to fit your own situation.

Because batch files can display text that you have entered into them, you can compose screens that help you execute a command, that contain syntax examples and reminders, or even just display a message of the day. Batch files can use the TYPE command to display text from a file.

In their advanced form, batch files can resemble computer programs. In this chapter you'll learn about simpler, yet useful forms of batch files. If batch processing interests you, be sure to read about batch files in the *MS-DOS User's Guide,* 3rd Ed.

Key Terms Used in This Chapter

Batch file	A text file that contains DOS commands, which DOS executes as though the commands were entered at the DOS prompt. Batch files always have a BAT extension.
Meta-string	A series of characters that takes on a different meaning to DOS than the literal meaning. DOS displays substitute text when it finds meta-strings in the PROMPT command.
AUTOEXEC.BAT file	An optional, but often included, batch file that is located in the root directory of a boot disk. AUTOEXEC.BAT is an ideal place to include commands that initialize the operation of a PC.
CONFIG.SYS file	A file whose contents are used by DOS to tailor hardware devices and allocate the computer's resources.
Buffer	An area of RAM allocated by DOS as a temporary storage area for data that is moving between the disks and an executing program.
Directive	A command-like DOS element that establishes the status or value of a system setting that can be modified. Unlike commands, directives don't execute. Rather, they set values.

Creating a Batch File

Batch files contain ASCII text characters. You can create a text file with many word processing programs in nondocument mode. *Nondocument mode* is a setting that omits special formatting and control characters which word-processing programs use for internal purposes. Composing batch files in nondocument mode eliminates errors in syntax that the special characters might cause.

You also may use the DOS line editor, EDLIN, to create a batch file. The easiest way to create a batch file, however, is to use the COPY CON device.

Caution: Never pick a name for your batch file that is the same as a DOS internal or external command. If you do, DOS will run the command instead of the batch file.

General Rules for Batch Files

When you create batch files, you must follow certain rules. The following list is a summary of those rules.

1. Batch files must be ASCII text files. If you use a word processor, be sure that it is in programming, or nondocument, mode.
2. The name of the batch file can be from one to eight characters long. The name must conform to the rules for naming files. It is best to use alphabetical characters in batch file names.
3. The file name must end with the BAT extension.
4. The batch file name should not be the same as a program file name (a file with an EXE or COM extension).
5. The batch file name should not be the same as an internal DOS command (such as COPY or DATE).
6. The batch file can contain any valid DOS commands that you might enter at the DOS prompt.

7. You can include program names in the batch file that you usually type at the DOS prompt.

8. Use only one command or program name per line in the batch file.

Rules for Running Batch Files

You start batch files by typing the batch file name (excluding the extension) at the DOS prompt. The following list summarizes the rules DOS follows when it loads and executes batch files.

1. If you do not specify the disk drive name before the batch file name, DOS uses the current drive.

2. If you do not give a path, DOS searches through the current directory for the batch file.

3. If the batch file is not in the current directory, and you did not precede the batch file name with a path, DOS searches the directories specified by the last PATH command you issued.

4. If DOS encounters a syntax error in a batch file command line, DOS displays an error message, skips the errant command, and executes the remaining commands in the batch file.

5. You can stop a batch command with Ctrl-C or Ctrl-Break. DOS will prompt you to confirm that you want to terminate the batch file. If you answer no, DOS skips the current command (the one being carried out) and resumes execution with the next command in the batch file.

If you try to run a batch file and DOS displays an error message, you probably made a mistake when you typed the name. You can view any batch file by using the **TYPE filename** command.

Creating a Batch File

Using COPY CON, create a batch file that clears the screen and presents a wide directory. This batch file automates the CLS screen clear command and the DIR command with the /W (wide display) switch.

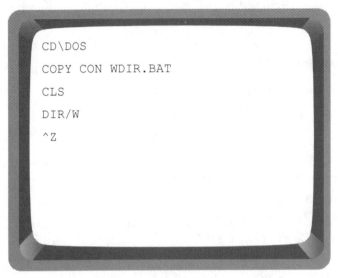

```
CD\DOS

COPY CON WDIR.BAT

CLS

DIR/W

^Z
```

1. If you have a hard disk, use the CD command to change to the directory that contains your DOS external commands.

2. Type **COPY CON WDIR.BAT** and press Enter. The cursor will drop to the next line, and DOS will wait for your keyboard input.

   Make sure that you type each line correctly. Use the backspace key to correct mistakes and then press Enter. If you do make a mistake and press Enter, press Ctrl-C and resume the process from this step.

3. Type **CLS** and press Enter.

4. Type **DIR/W** and press Enter.

5. Type Ctrl-Z (hold down the Ctrl key and type Z) or press the F6 function key.

6. Press Enter.

   DOS will display the message 1 File(s) Copied.

   To see that the directory contains the new batch file, type **DIR WDIR.BAT** and press Enter. To try out the batch file, type **WDIR** and press Enter. The screen will clear and the directory will display in its wide form. You have just created a new DOS batch file using COPY CON!

210

Creating a batch file using a word-processing program is even easier than using COPY CON.

```
CLS
DIR/W
```

1. Start your word-processing program.

2. Create a nondocument file, making sure the file name has the BAT extension.

3. Type **CLS** and press Enter.

4. Type **DIR/W**.

5. Save your nondocument.

   To try out the batch file, type **WDIR** at the system prompt and press Enter. The screen will clear and the directory will display in its wide form. You have just created a new DOS batch file using your word processor!

Understanding the AUTOEXEC.BAT File

One batch file has special significance to DOS. The full name of this batch file is *AUTOEXEC.BAT*. DOS automatically searches for this file in the root directory when you boot your computer. If an AUTOEXEC.BAT file is present, DOS executes the commands in the file.

Because the AUTOEXEC.BAT file is optional, not every PC has this file. However, most users or their system managers include an AUTOEXEC.BAT file of their own design on their boot disk because it allows them to benefit from commands that establish operating parameters automatically.

You could elect to omit AUTOEXEC.BAT, enter manually the commands you might include in an AUTOEXEC.BAT file, and accomplish the same result as an AUTOEXEC.BAT file. But since DOS will execute the file if it is there, why not take advantage? As a rule, AUTOEXEC.BAT files are not distributed with the DOS package because different users need varied commands.

The installation process for DOS V4.0 creates a file called AUTOEXEC.400, which includes commands that the user might want. By changing the name of the AUTOEXEC.400 file to AUTOEXEC.BAT, you enable DOS to execute the commands in the file after booting.

Some software programs come with installation programs that create or modify AUTOEXEC.BAT as one of the installation steps for the package's main program. If you have doubts about what commands you should include in your AUTOEXEC.BAT file, the following sections will give you some ideas.

You can include any commands you want in the AUTOEXEC.BAT file. Then when you boot your computer, DOS executes those commands.

You can decide what you want the AUTOEXEC.BAT file to do, as long as you follow certain rules. The following list is a summary of these rules.

1. The full file name must be AUTOEXEC.BAT and the file must reside in the root directory of the boot disk.
2. The contents of the AUTOEXEC.BAT file must conform to the rules for creating any batch file.
3. When DOS executes AUTOEXEC.BAT after a boot, you are not prompted for the date and time automatically. You must include the DATE and TIME commands in your AUTOEXEC.BAT file if you want to retain this step in booting.

Using AUTOEXEC.BAT is a great way for you to set up changeable system defaults. That is, AUTOEXEC.BAT is the place to put commands you would want to enter every time you start your system. For example, you can use AUTOEXEC.BAT to tell your computer to change to the directory that holds your most commonly used program and start the program. Used in this way, AUTOEXEC.BAT starts your program as soon as you boot your computer.

Table 10.1 lists the commands most frequently included in simple AUTOEXEC.BAT files.

Table 10.1
AUTOEXEC.BAT File Commands

Command	Function in the AUTOEXEC.BAT File
TIME DATE	These commands establish the correct time and date so that DOS can accurately "stamp" new and modified files. They also provide the actual time and date to programs that use the computer's internal clock.

Understanding the AUTOEXEC.BAT File

Table 10.1
AUTOEXEC.BAT File Commands *(continued)*

Command	*Function in the AUTOEXEC.BAT File*
PATH	Eliminates the need for the operator to enter the path through the keyboard after each boot.
PROMPT	Customizes the system prompt. The DOS prompt configuration can include information that makes navigating in directories easier. If you use the PROMPT command in the AUTOEXEC.BAT file, you don't need to remember how to input the optional parameters each time you boot.
DIR CD	Shows a listing of the root directory as soon as the computer boots. When used with a directory path, CD takes you immediately to a directory where you normally do your work.
ECHO	Allows you to include a message as part of your start-up when used in the AUTOEXEC.BAT file. On a floppy disk system, this message could remind you to insert a program disk in drive A.

The PATH Command

You know how to issue the PATH command to tell DOS where to search for .COM, .EXE, and .BAT files. In this section, you learn how to put the PATH command that contains the search paths into the AUTOEXEC.BAT file. With this information, DOS will know the search path as soon as you boot the computer. For example, suppose that you create a directory on your hard disk called \DOS. To tell DOS to search the \DOS directory, you would type

PATH C:\DOS

If you want DOS to search in the root directory first, the \DOS directory next, and another directory—such as \TEMP—last, type

PATH C:\;C:\DOS;C:\TEMP

Notice that semicolons separate the three directory names. The path you include in the AUTOEXEC.BAT file becomes DOS's default search path. Of course, you can change this default path. Simply issue the PATH command with a new path or set of paths at the DOS prompt.

The PROMPT Command

You know what your DOS prompt looks like, but did you know that you can change it? With the PROMPT command, you can change the DOS prompt to a wide variety of looks. The symbolic syntax for the PROMPT command is

PROMPT *text*

The *text* is any combination of words or special characters. The term used to describe the special characters is *meta-strings*.

Meta-strings

A meta-string consists of two characters, the first of which is the dollar sign ($). DOS interprets meta-strings to mean something other than the literal meaning of the characters. For instance, the meta-string $T in the

215

Understanding the AUTOEXEC.BAT File

PROMPT command tells DOS, "My meaning is the current time in HH:MM:SS." Placed in the DOS prompt, $T prints the current system time.

DOS recognizes the symbols >, <, and the vertical bar (|) as special characters. They all have meta-string equivalents so that you can use them in PROMPT text. You must substitute the appropriate meta-string in order to cause these special characters to appear in the prompt. Otherwise, DOS tries to act on the characters in its usual way.

The following list summarizes meta-string characters and their meanings to the PROMPT command.

Table 10.2
Meta-string Characters

Character	What it Produces
$	$, the actual dollar sign
_(underscore)	moves the cursor to the next line
B	the vertical bar |
D	the current date
G	the > character
L	the < character
N	the current disk drive name
P	the current drive and path
Q	the = character
T	the system time
V	the DOS version
Any other	the character is ignored

Customizing Your Prompt

You can use the meta-string characters with the PROMPT command to produce your own DOS prompt. PROMPT allows words or phrases in addition to meta-strings. You can experiment with different combinations of meta-strings and phrases. When you find a combination that you favor, type the PROMPT command and the meta-string and phrase. Then, each time you boot your computer your custom prompt will appear. Issuing the PROMPT command alone with no parameters restores the prompt to its default, which is the drive name and the greater-than sign (C>).

If you want your prompt to tell you the current DOS path, type the command

PROMPT THE CURRENT PATH IS $P

If your current location were on drive C in the DOS directory, this PROMPT command would produce the following prompt:

```
THE CURRENT PATH IS C:\DOS
```

By adding the > sign (using the meta-string $G), the command would be

PROMPT THE CURRENT PATH IS PG

Now your DOS prompt would appear as:

```
THE CURRENT PATH IS C:\DOS>
```

Understanding the AUTOEXEC.BAT File

AUTOEXEC.BAT — A batch file whose commands DOS
executes each time you boot the computer.

```
DATE
TIME
PATH=C:\DOS;C:\KEEP;C:\;
PROMPT $P$G
DIR
CD\DOS
ECHO Good Day, Mate
```

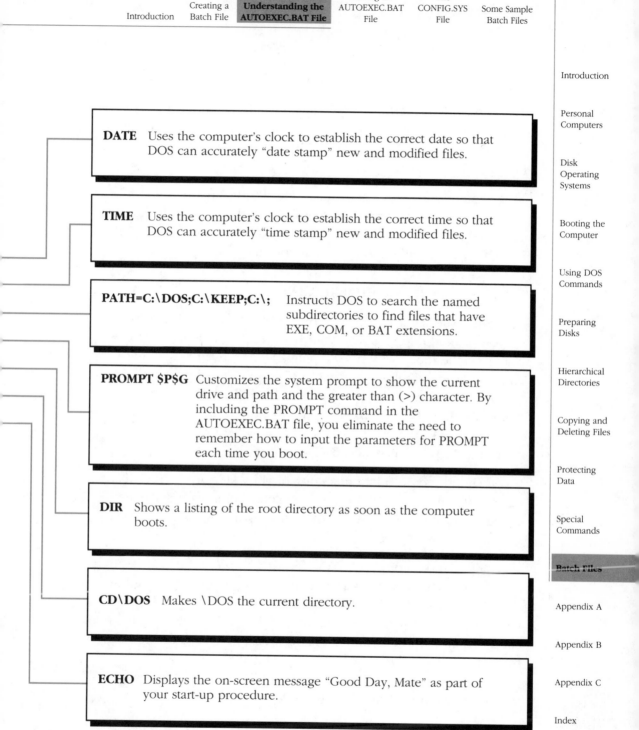

DATE Uses the computer's clock to establish the correct date so that DOS can accurately "date stamp" new and modified files.

TIME Uses the computer's clock to establish the correct time so that DOS can accurately "time stamp" new and modified files.

PATH=C:\DOS;C:\KEEP;C:\; Instructs DOS to search the named subdirectories to find files that have EXE, COM, or BAT extensions.

PROMPT PG Customizes the system prompt to show the current drive and path and the greater than (>) character. By including the PROMPT command in the AUTOEXEC.BAT file, you eliminate the need to remember how to input the parameters for PROMPT each time you boot.

DIR Shows a listing of the root directory as soon as the computer boots.

CD\DOS Makes \DOS the current directory.

ECHO Displays the on-screen message "Good Day, Mate" as part of your start-up procedure.

Making an AUTOEXEC.BAT File

The AUTOEXEC.BAT file is a privileged batch file because DOS executes its batch of commands each time you boot your computer. In every other sense, however, AUTOEXEC.BAT is like any other batch file.

Most computers already have an AUTOEXEC.BAT file in the root directory of the hard disk or on the bootable floppy disk. In addition, packaged software sometimes creates or adds to the AUTOEXEC.BAT file when you install the software on your hard disk.

If You Already Have AUTOEXEC.BAT

You can easily see if AUTOEXEC.BAT exists in your root directory or on your logged floppy disk. If your hard disk is the logged drive, change to the root directory by typing **CD**. You can look at the directory listing of all the files with .BAT extensions by typing **DIR *.BAT**. You can view the contents of AUTOEXEC.BAT on-screen by typing **TYPE AUTOEXEC.BAT**. You also can get a printed copy of the AUTOEXEC.BAT file by redirecting output to the printer with the command **TYPE AUTOEXEC.BAT >PRN**.

If you choose not to print out a copy of your AUTOEXEC.BAT file, make sure that you write down the contents before you make any changes. Be sure that you copy the syntax correctly. This copy will serve as your worksheet.

You can use your copy of AUTOEXEC.BAT to see if a PROMPT or PATH command is contained in the batch file. If you want to add or alter PROMPT or PATH commands, jot the additions or changes on your worksheet. Use your paper copy of the AUTOEXEC.BAT file to check for proper syntax in the lines you change or add before you commit the changes to disk.

Making a Backup of the Existing File

Always make a backup copy of your existing AUTOEXEC.BAT file before you make any changes in the file. Save the current version by renaming it with a different extension. Type the command

RENAME AUTOEXEC.BAT AUTOEXEC.OLD

and press Enter. RENAME transfers the name AUTOEXEC.BAT to the AUTOEXEC.OLD file. In effect, the name AUTOEXEC.BAT is available for use with a new file. If you find that the new AUTOEXEC.BAT file does not work or does not do what you want, you can always erase the new file. Then, using the RENAME command, you can rename the AUTOEXEC.OLD file AUTOEXEC.BAT and be back where you started.

Entering the New File

Now you are ready to use COPY CON to enter your new or revised AUTOEXEC.BAT file. Type the command **COPY CON AUTOEXEC.BAT**. Enter the commands from your worksheet. Type one command per line and correct any mistakes before you press Enter. When you finish, press F6 or Ctrl-Z to write the new file to disk. Now when you boot your computer, DOS executes your new AUTOEXEC.BAT file.

Keeping Several Versions of AUTOEXEC

Technically speaking, there is only one AUTOEXEC.BAT file. But you can have the benefit of several "versions" by giving different extensions to files with the name AUTOEXEC. You can then activate an alternative version by using the RENAME and COPY commands.

You can use in the extensions any character that DOS normally allows in file names. The extensions .BAK, .OLD, .NEW, TMP, and .001 are just a few examples. By giving AUTOEXEC.BAT a unique new name such as AUTOEXEC.TMP, you can activate any other AUTOEXEC file by renaming it AUTOEXEC.BAT.

This method is handy if you want to include commands for some activity such as automatically starting a monthly spreadsheet. When the monthly work is done, and you no longer need to concentrate on the spreadsheet as soon as you boot, you can activate your normal AUTOEXEC.BAT file by changing its temporary name back to AUTOEXEC.BAT.

Making an AUTOEXEC.BAT File

```
CD\
DIR *.BAT
```

Use the DIR command to check for the presence of an AUTOEXEC.BAT file.

```
TYPE AUTOEXEC.BAT
```

Display on-screen the contents of the AUTOEXEC.BAT file using the TYPE command.

```
REN AUTOEXEC.BAT AUTOEXEC.OLD
```

Save a copy of the original AUTOEXEC.BAT file under the new name AUTOEXEC.OLD.

```
COPY CON AUTOEXEC.BAT
DATE
TIME
PATH=C:\DOS;C:\KEEP;C:\
CD\DOS
^Z
```

Create a new AUTOEXEC.BAT file using COPY CON.

Ctrl Alt Del   When you reboot, DOS executes the commands in the new AUTOEXEC.BAT file. You can also run the AUTOEXEC.BAT file by typing **AUTOEXEC** at the system prompt.

```
ERASE AUTOEXEC.BAT
REN AUTOEXEC.OLD AUTOEXEC.BAT
```

Remember that the contents of the AUTOEXEC.OLD file are the original AUTOEXEC.BAT file. To get back to where you started, erase the current AUTOEXEC.BAT; then use the RENAME command to change the name AUTOEXEC.OLD to AUTOEXEC.BAT.

The CONFIG.SYS File

AUTOEXEC.BAT is not the only file that DOS looks for when you boot your computer. DOS also looks for *CONFIG.SYS*. CONFIG.SYS is DOS's additional configuration file. Not only does DOS provide built-in services for disks and other hardware, it also extends its services for add-on hardware. The additional instructions that DOS needs to incorporate outside services, such as some devices, are included in the CONFIG.SYS file.

CONFIG.SYS is also the location for naming the values of DOS configuration items that can be "tuned." Files and buffers, which are discussed in the next section, are two "tunable" DOS items. CONFIG.SYS is a text file like AUTOEXEC.BAT, so you can display it on-screen or print it. You can also change the contents of CONFIG.SYS with the COPY CON command or with a text editor.

Although CONFIG.SYS is not a batch file, it is very similar to one. DOS does not execute CONFIG.SYS as it does AUTOEXEC.BAT. Instead, DOS reads the values in the file and configures your computer in accordance with those values. Many software packages modify or add a CONFIG.SYS file to the root directory. The range of possible values in the file is wide, but there are some common values that you can include.

Files and Buffers

When DOS moves data to and from disks, it does so in the most efficient manner possible. For each file that DOS works with during an operation, there is a built-in area in system RAM that helps DOS keep track of the operating system details of that file. The number of built-in RAM areas for this tracking operation is controlled by the FILES directive in CONFIG.SYS. (A *directive* establishes in the CONFIG.SYS file the value of a system setting that can be modified.) If a program attempts to open more files than the FILES directive indicates, DOS will tell you too many files are open.

Do not be be tempted to set your FILES directive to a large number so that you will always have room for more open files. The system RAM for programs is reduced by each extra file included in FILES. As a rule of thumb, the best compromise is 20 open files. The line you type in CONFIG.SYS to set the number of open files to 20 is

FILES=20

Similar to the FILES directive is the BUFFERS directive. *Buffers* are holding areas in RAM that store information coming from or going to disk files. To make the disk operation more efficient, DOS stores disk information in file buffers in RAM. It then uses RAM, instead of the disk drives, for input and output whenever possible. If the file information needed is not already in the buffer, new information is read into the buffer from the disk file. The information that DOS reads includes the needed information and as much additional file information as the buffer will hold. With this buffer of needed information, there is a good chance that DOS can avoid constant disk access. The principle is similar to the way a mechanic might use a small tool pouch as a buffer. Holding tools that are frequently used in a small pouch keeps him from having to make numerous trips across the garage to get tools from his main tool chest.

Like the FILES directive, however, setting the BUFFERS directive too high takes needed RAM away from programs and dedicates it to the buffers. As a rule, 20 buffers should work effectively for you.

To include the FILES and BUFFERS directives in the CONFIG.SYS file during the COPY CON command, type **FILES=20** and press Enter. Then type **BUFFERS=20** on the next line. Keep in mind that some programs make their own changes to FILES and BUFFERS in the CONFIG.SYS file. Most applications software tells you what the values of FILES and BUFFERS should be. Check your program manual for details.

You can use FILES and BUFFERS settings above 20 with DOS 3.3 and 4.0, but as a general rule, do not use a setting of more than 20 unless the program documentation instructs you to.

The CONFIG.SYS File

Device Drivers

You'll recall that DOS works with peripherals, such as disk drives, printers, and displays. These peripherals are also called devices. DOS has built-in instructions, called *drivers*, to handle these devices. But some devices, like a mouse, are foreign to DOS. DOS does not have any built-in capability to handle them. To issue directions to devices DOS has no built-in instructions for, use the DEVICE directive. The syntax for the directive is

DEVICE= *device driver file name*

For example, the device driver for a mouse can be in a file called MOUSE.SYS. So that DOS can know how to use the mouse, you would enter a command like this:

DEVICE= MOUSE.SYS

The DEVICE directive tells DOS to find and load the driver program for the new device. Then, DOS can control the device.

Most peripherals come with a disk that contains a device-driver file. This file contains the necessary instructions to control or drive the device. The device-driver disk usually contains a provision to modify your CONFIG.SYS file to include the proper DEVICE directive. The device driver is often copied from the device's installation disk to a new subdirectory that the installation program creates. The DEVICE directive will then include the full path to the driver so that DOS can locate it.

If you copy a device driver file to its own subdirectory, use the full path to the driver file when you put the DEVICE directive in CONFIG.SYS. For example, suppose that you install a Microsoft™ Mouse device driver called MOUSE.SYS in a directory named \DOS\DRIVERS. You would add the following line in your CONFIG.SYS file:

DEVICE = \DOS\DRIVERS\MOUSE.SYS

Introduction

Creating a
Batch File

Understanding the
AUTOEXEC.BAT File

Making an
AUTOEXEC.BAT
File

The
CONFIG.SYS
File

Some Sample
Batch Files

This directive allows your mouse to start working when you boot. Always check your program and hardware manuals before experimenting with your system. Many programs provide prepared device directives for you.

Making a CONFIG.SYS File

You should back up your disk before you add to or change a CONFIG.SYS file. Make sure that the CONFIG.SYS file is in your root directory, or on your boot floppy. If your directory contains CONFIG.SYS, use the TYPE command to see the contents of the file on the screen. If you have a printer, you can redirect the TYPE command's output to the printer. Use the printout or a written copy of the CONFIG.SYS file as a worksheet to write the directives you want to change or include.

If you need to change your CONFIG.SYS file, rename it CONFIG.OLD. Now you can use the command COPY CON CONFIG.SYS to make a new version. Type your directives from your worksheet and pay close attention to syntax. When you finish, press F6 or Ctrl-Z. Reboot your computer. The new configuration will take effect. If you get DOS error messages, TYPE your new CONFIG.SYS and check for mistakes. If you find errors, erase the file and use COPY CON to type the lines again. A sample CONFIG.SYS file might contain these lines:

FILES=20
BUFFERS=20
DEVICE=\DOS\DRIVERS\ANSI.SYS
DEVICE=\DOS\DRIVERS\MOUSE.SYS

Your CONFIG.SYS might contain other device drivers and DOS settings. Because the subdirectories on each computer may vary, the exact contents of CONFIG.SYS device directives will vary. If you want to explore configurations and device concepts in more detail, consult the *MS-DOS User's Guide,* 3rd Ed. If you are unsure about the device drivers for new peripherals you buy, ask your dealer how to incorporate the new device.

227

The CONFIG.SYS File

CONFIG.SYS — A DOS configuration file that is used for naming the values of DOS configuration items that can be "tuned."

```
FILES=20
BUFFERS=20
DEVICE=\DOS\DRIVERS\MOUSE.SYS
DEVICE=\DOS\DRIVERS\ANSI.SYS
```

FILES=20   Establishes 20 built-in RAM areas for DOS to keep track of the operating-system details of open files. If a program you use tries to open more than 20 files, DOS will tell you too many files are open.

BUFFERS=20   Sets up 20 holding areas in RAM that store information coming from or going to disk files. DOS then uses RAM, instead of the disk drives, for input and output whenever possible.

DEVICE=\DOS\DRIVERS\MOUSE.SYS   Tells DOS how to handle a peripheral device, in this case, a mouse.

DEVICE=\DOS\DRIVERS\ANSI.SYS   American National Standards Institute screen-control character sequences.

229

Some Sample Batch Files

If you are a beginner, you may benefit from entering sample batch files. Practicing with the following examples will make it easier to understand DOS batch files.

Simplified Backup Using a Batch File

You know how important it is to back up your files. Perhaps a batch file that issues the command to back up your entire hard disk would be useful. You can execute this batch file once per month or bi-weekly to keep a snapshot of your hard disk.

This batch file uses the ECHO command to send text to your display. ECHO OFF stops the echoing of the DOS commands in the file. Using ECHO OFF keeps the screen uncluttered by the commands as the file executes. It does, however, allow text to display as the result of an ECHO command. The PAUSE command is used to hold the execution of the batch file until you press a key. Using the COPY CON method, create the following file in your DOS disk or directory:

```
COPY CON BIGBACK.BAT
ECHO OFF
CLS
ECHO  ********************************************************************
ECHO *                                                                  *
ECHO *  YOU ARE ABOUT TO INITIATE A FULL BACKUP OF YOUR HARD DISK       *
ECHO *                                                                  *
ECHO *  You will be asked to insert floppy disks into drive A.          *
ECHO *                                                                  *
ECHO *  Please have your floppies ready before proceeding.              *
ECHO *                                                                  *
ECHO *  IF YOU DON'T WANT TO PROCEED, ENTER Ctrl-C TO STOP              *
ECHO *  AND ANSWER 'Y' TO THE TERMINATION PROMPT THAT WILL             *
ECHO *  FOLLOW CTRL C.                                                  *
ECHO *                                                                  *
ECHO  ********************************************************************
ECHO ^G (entered as Ctrl+G on keyboard to produce a beep)
PAUSE
CLS
ECHO ** FULL HARD DISK BACKUP IN PROGRESS. . .  Ctrl-C to Stop       **
ECHO ON
\DOS\BACKUP C:\*.* A:/S
ECHO OFF
CLS
ECHO **           THE FULL BACKUP OPERATION HAS TERMINATED            **
ECHO **              YOU HAVE RETURNED TO THE DOS PROMPT              **
ECHO ON
F6 Key or Ctrl Z
```

You now have in your DOS directory the batch file BIGBACK. This file does a complete backup after you provide some start-up information. If you want to verify the file, use the TYPE command to send the file to the screen or use redirection to print the file.

A Batch File To Display Help Text

Using the batch-file provisions of DOS does not mean that you can only include commands that do DOS jobs. You can also include commands that provide information for you or another user. In this example, text information is echoed to the screen. The text provides you help for the COPY command. You can substitute your own help text for another DOS command using the same method.

This batch file is called COPYHELP.BAT. If you include it in your current directory, you can see the text by typing COPYHELP. Type the file as follows:

```
COPY CON > COPYHELP.BAT
ECHO OFF
CLS
ECHO **                    COPY COMMAND HELP INFORMATION            **
ECHO *                                                              *
ECHO *  FULL SYNTAX: COPY sd:sp\sf.ext (space) dd:dp\df.ext /V      *
ECHO *  s=Source, d=Drive Letter, p=Path Name, d=Destination       *
ECHO *  f.ext=Filename and Extension.     /V=Verify Switch          *
ECHO *  A Space separates the Source and Destination file parameters. *
ECHO *                                                              *
ECHO *        FILES ARE COPIED FROM SOURCE TO DESTINATION.          *
ECHO *   ? wildcard matches any character and * matches all characters. *
ECHO *   Wildcards allow copying of all files that match the command line. *
ECHO *                                                              *
ECHO *  If the source or destination drive or path is the current drive *
ECHO *  or path, that parameter may be omitted.  (Rule of Currents) *
ECHO *                                                              *
ECHO *                   ---COPY EXAMPLES---                        *
ECHO *                                                              *
ECHO *  (1)COPY A:*.* C:  (2)COPY \TEMP\MYFILE.123  \KEEP\YOURFILE.XYZ /V *
ECHO *  (3)COPY MEMO.DOC MEMO.BAK (4)COPY CON AUTOEXEC.BAT (redirection) *
ECHO *                                                              *
ECHO **                                                             **
ECHO ON
F6 Key or Ctrl Z
```

Appendix A

This *Command Reference* includes the most frequently used MS-DOS commands. Each command is presented in the same format: the command name appears first, followed by either the notation ⊡ Internal or ⊡ External. These graphics indicate whether the command is built into MS-DOS (internal) or is disk-resident (external). Next, the command's purpose is explained, followed by the syntax required to invoke the command. Finally, a set of step-by-step instructions for using the command appears.

External Commands

You recall that DOS's internal commands may be issued from any disk drive or directory. Issuing external commands is a bit more complex. To issue an external command, you have three alternatives:

1. Change to the directory that holds the external command.
2. Include the path name (disk drive, if necessary, and directory name) each time you issue the command. This technique can quickly become tedious.
3. Be sure that the directory that holds the external command is included in the last PATH command you issued.

If you try to issue a command and get a `Bad command or file name` message, you don't have the path set with the PATH command or the command is not in the default directory on the logged disk drive. Remember the rule of currents for issuing commands:

1. If you do not give a disk drive name for the command, MS-DOS will search for the command on the current disk drive.
2. If you do not give a path, MS-DOS will search for the command on the current directory of the current disk (or the current directory of the specified disk drive if one was given).

A Note about Notation

In the command notation used in this appendix, *d:* is the name of the disk drive holding the file, and *path* is the directory path to the file. *filename* is the root name of the file, and *.ext* is the file name extension.

If any part of this notation does not appear in the syntax for the command, the omitted part is not allowed with that command. For example, the notation *d:filename.ext* indicates that path names are not allowed in the command.

Commands that use source and destination drive parameters use *sd:* for the source drive name and *dd:* for the destination (target) drive name. *s* and *d* parameters are also used for other commands in some instances.

233

BACKUP

 External

Use BACKUP To:

Back up hard disk information to protect original programs and data in case of loss or damage.

Back up files created or altered since a specific date or since the last backup.

Copy long files that cannot be stored on one floppy disk.

Command Syntax

BACKUP *sd:spath\sfilename.ext dd: /switches*

Follow These Steps

1. Type BACKUP and press the space bar once. You may need to precede the command with a drive and path for BACKUP.COM because BACKUP is an external command.

2. Type the drive name of the hard disk to be backed up (*sd*). For example, type C: if you are backing up drive C. To back up only a directory or an individual file, type the path, file name, and extension; then press the space bar. You can use wild-card characters (* and ?) to designate groups of files.

3. Type the name of the drive that will receive the backup files (*dd*). For example, if you are backing up on a floppy disk in drive A, type A:.

4. Use any of the following optional switches with the BACKUP command:

/S   backs up the subdirectories as well as the current directory. If you start at the root directory, DOS will back up all subdirectories.

/M   backs up files modified since the last backup. Use the /A switch with the /M switch to avoid erasing unmodified files when restoring from the backup disks. These switches are used in incremental backups.

/A   adds files to the files already on the backup disk.

/D: mm-dd-yy instructs DOS to back up files created or changed on or after a particular date.

/T: hh:mm:ss instructs DOS to back up files created or changed at or after a particular time (V3.3 and later).

/F   formats the target floppy disk (V.3.3 only).

5. Press Enter.

CHDIR or CD

Use CHDIR or CD To:

Change the current directory.

Show the name of the current directory.

Command Syntax

CHDIR *d:path*

or

CD *d:path*

Follow These Steps

1. Type CHDIR. CHDIR (CD) is an internal command that does not require a path.
2. Press the space bar.
3. Type the drive name of the disk whose current directory is to be changed (for example, A:, B:, C:, etc.) and the name of the directory you want to change to. If you don't specify a path, the current path will be displayed. Don't forget to use the backslash to separate the parts of the path.
4. Press Enter.

CHKDSK

 External

Use CHKDSK To:

Check the directory of the disk for disk and memory status. CHKDSK can show:

> the number of files and directories on a disk
>
> the bytes used and the space available on a disk
>
> the presence of hidden files
>
> whether a floppy disk is bootable
>
> the total RAM and available RAM
>
> whether files are fragmented (non-contiguous)
>
> CHKDSK can also make minor repairs.

Command Syntax

CHKDSK *d:path\filename.ext* /F/V

Follow These Steps

1. Type CHKDSK and press the space bar. You may need to precede the command with a drive and path for CHKDSK (the optional *d:path* in the syntax), because CHKDSK is an external command.

2. If you want to check a disk on another drive, type the drive name after CHKDSK. If your default drive is A, and you want to check drive B, you would type CHKDSK B:

3. You can use CHKDSK to determine the noncontiguous areas in an individual file by entering the path, file name, and extension. The filename and extension can contain wild cards.

4. Specify optional switches:

   /F repairs errors (use with caution).

   /V = verbose; and displays paths and file names.

5. Press Enter.

CLS

| $*$ | Internal |

Use CLS To:

Clear the screen whenever you are at the DOS prompt.

Command Syntax

CLS

Follow These Steps

1. Type CLS
2. Press Enter. After all messages on-screen are cleared, the DOS prompt and the cursor reappear in the upper left corner.

COPY

Use COPY To:

Copy one or more files to another disk or directory, or copy a file to the same directory and change its name.

Transfer information between DOS system devices.

Send text to the printer.

Create ASCII text files and batch files.

Command Syntax

The most common syntax for the COPY command is

COPY *sd:\path\filename.ext dd:\path\filename.ext /switches*

Follow These Steps

1. Type COPY and press the space bar.
2. Type the optional drive name and path of the source file (*sd:\path*).
3. Type the name of the file to be copied. Wild cards are allowed.
4. You can include the following switches for the source file:

   /A treats the source file as an ASCII text file.

   /B forces the entire file to be copied as though it were a program file (binary). Binary copying is the default value.
5. Press the space bar.
6. Type the optional drive name, path, and file name of the target file (*dd:\path*). Skip this step if the file name is to remain the same as that of the source file.

7. You may include the following switches for the target file.

   /A places a Ctrl-Z (end-of-file character) at the end of the copied file.

   /B prevents a Ctrl-Z from being added to a copied file.

8. You may add a /V switch to verify and check the accuracy of the COPY procedure.

9. Press Enter.

Command Reference

DATE

Use DATE To:

Enter or change the system date.

Set the internal clock on Personal Computer ATs and PS/2 computers.

Insure the current date-stamp for newly created and modified files.

Provide control for programs that require date information, such as BACKUP and RESTORE.

Command Syntax

DATE date_format

Follow These Steps

1. Type DATE and press the space bar.
2. Enter the date in one of the three following formats:

   mm-dd-yy (for North America; this is the default)

   dd-mm-yy (for Europe)

   yy-mm-dd or yyyy-mm-dd (for East Asia)

   mm is a one- or two-digit number for the month (1 to 12).

   dd is a one- or two-digit number for the day (1 to 31).

   yy is a one- or two-digit number for the year (80 to 99). The 19 is assumed.

   yyyy is a four-digit number for the year (1980 to 2099).

   You can separate the entries with hyphens, periods, or slashes.
3. Press Enter.

DEVICE

 Internal

Use DEVICE To:

> Support add-on peripherals.
>
> Install a block-device driver.
>
> Install a virtual (RAM) Disk.

Command Syntax

> DEVICE= device driver filename

Follow These Steps

1. Using a text editor, open your CONFIG.SYS file. If you do not have a CONFIG.SYS file, create one with COPY CON or with a text editor.

2. Type on one line in your CONFIG.SYS file the command DEVICE=device driver filename

3. Repeat Step 2 until all desired device drivers are included in your CONFIG.SYS file.

4. Restart your system.

Note: Device drivers usually come with hardware you purchase. Check installation instructions for your device and driver.

DIR

Use DIR To:

Display a list of files and subdirectories in a disk's directory.

List a specified group of files within a directory.

Examine the volume identification label of the disk.

Determine the amount of available space on the disk.

Check the size of individual files.

Check the date the files were last modified.

Command Syntax

DIR d:\path\filename.ext /W/P

Follow These Steps

1. Type DIR and press the space bar.
2. You can also type

   The drive name whose directory you want displayed;

   The path name whose directory you want displayed;

   The file name if you want to limit the number and types of files to be listed. You can use wild cards to list groups of files.
3. Specify optional switches:

   /W displays the directory in a wide format of five columns across. Only the directory name and file names will be displayed. For large listings, you can also include the /P switch.

   /P displays the directory and pauses between screen pages. This switch prevents large directories from scrolling past the screen before you can read them.
4. Press Enter.

DISKCOMP

→💾 External

Use DISKCOMP To:

Compare two floppy disks on a track-for-track, sector-for-sector basis to see whether their contents are identical.

Verify the integrity of a DISKCOPY operation.

Command Syntax

DISKCOMP *source d: destination d:*

Follow These Steps

Dual Disk Drives:

1. Type DISKCOMP and press the space bar.
2. Type the name of the drive that holds the source disk (for example, type A:) and press the space bar again.
3. Type the name of the drive that holds the target disk (for example, B:).
4. Press Enter, and you will be instructed to place the source disk into drive A and the target disk into drive B.
5. Insert the disks and press Enter again. DISKCOMP will compare all tracks and issue any necessary error messages, indicating the track number and side of the disk where errors occur. When DISKCOMP has finished, you will be asked whether you want to compare more disks.
6. Press Y or N. If you press Y, repeat steps 4, 5, and 6.

Command Reference

Single Disk Drive:

1. Type DISKCOMP and press the space bar.
2. Press Enter. A prompt will appear instructing you to place the source disk in drive A.
3. Insert the disk and press Enter once more. After a minute or two, a second prompt will instruct you to insert the target disk in drive A:.
4. Insert the disk and press Enter again.
5. Continue swapping disks as prompted until DOS finishes comparing the disks. When the comparison is complete, you will be asked whether you want to compare another disk.
6. Press either Y or N. If you press Y, repeat Steps 2,3, and 4.

DISKCOPY

 External

Use DISKCOPY To:

> Secure data against loss by duplicating a floppy disk. Note that DISKCOPY works only with floppy disks.

Command Syntax

DISKCOPY *source d: destination d:*

Follow These Steps

Dual Disk Drives:

1. Type DISKCOPY and press the space bar.
2. Type the name of the drive that holds the source disk (A:, for example) and press the space bar once more.
3. Type the name of the drive that holds the target disk (B:, for example).
4. Press Enter. Within a few seconds, you will be prompted to place the source disk in drive A and the target disk into drive B.
5. Insert the disks and press Enter.
6. When the copy is complete, you will be asked whether you want to copy another disk.
7. Press either Y or N. If you press Y, repeat Steps 4, 5, and 6.

Command Reference

Single Disk Drive:

1. Type DISKCOPY.
3. Press Enter. Within a few seconds, you will be prompted to place the source disk in drive A.
4. Insert the source disk and press Enter. After a minute or two, you will be prompted to insert the target disk.
5. Place the blank target disk into drive A and press Enter.
6. Repeat Steps 3 and 4 until DOS finishes copying. You will then be asked whether you want to copy another disk.
7. Press either Y or N. If you press Y, repeat Steps 3 through 5.

ECHO

 Internal

Use ECHO To:

Display batch-file commands and text strings on the screen.
Control video output to the screen.
Debug batch files.

Command Syntax

To turn off the display of commands when you run batch files.

ECHO OFF

To turn on the display of commands

ECHO ON

To display a message:

ECHO *message*

ERASE or DEL

Use ERASE or DEL To:

Remove one or more files from the directory.

Command Syntax

ERASE d:path\filename.ext

or

DEL d:path\filename.ext

Follow These Steps

1. Type ERASE or DEL and press the space bar.
2. Type the drive name and path of the file to be deleted, unless the file is in the current directory.
3. Type the name of the file to be deleted.
4. Press Enter.

FIND

→🖫 External

Use FIND To:

> Display lines that contain, or fail to contain, a certain group of characters. These characters are called a string.

Command Syntax

FIND */C/N/V* "string" *d:path*\filename.ext. . .

Note that switches for FIND are placed in the middle of the command line, before the search string is specified.

Follow These Steps

1. Type FIND and press the space bar. Note that the FIND filter is an external file. FIND's location (disk drive and path) may need to precede the FIND command if FIND is not in the root directory or on a path governed by the PATH command.

2. Specify optional switches:

   /C counts the number of lines that contain the string being searched.

   /N displays the line number of each line that contains the string.

   /V displays lines that do not contain the search string.

3. Type the string, enclosed in double quotation marks ("string"). The string is the set of characters you will search for. FIND is case-sensitive. If you want to find uppercase characters, for example, the "string" must be typed in uppercase letters.

4. If the file is not in the current directory, type the drive name and path where the file being searched is located.

5. Type the file name and extension of the file to be searched.

6. Press the space bar and repeat Steps 4 and 5 for each file you want FIND to search. You cannot use wild-card characters (? or *).

7. Press Enter.

FORMAT

| →🖫 | External |

Use FORMAT To:

> Initialize a floppy disk or hard disk to accept DOS information and files.

Command Syntax

> FORMAT d: /S /1 /8 /V /B /4 N:xx T:xx

Follow These Steps

1. Type FORMAT.
2. Press the space bar.
3. Type the name of the drive that will hold the floppy disk to be formatted, for drive B, type **B:**.
4. Select optional switches:

    /V gives the formatted disk a unique, identifying volume label.

    /S produces a bootable floppy disk with the DOS operating system on the formatted disk.

    /4 formats, on a high-capacity drive, a single-sided or double-sided floppy disk to be used in computers that use double-density disks.

    /1 formats a disk on one side. Use this switch to format minifloppy disks for older PCs and compatibles.

    /8 formats a floppy disk with eight sectors per track instead of the default value of nine sectors per track. Use to format disks for older PCs and compatibles.

/B creates an eight-sector floppy disk that will reserve space for the operating system.

/N:xx formats a disk with a different number of sectors than the default value. xx represents the number of sectors. Always use this switch with the /T:xx switch.

/T:xx specifies a different number of tracks to format. xx represents the number of tracks. Use this switch with the /N:xx switch.

5. Press Enter.

6. DOS now instructs you to place a floppy disk into the drive you named in Step 3. Insert the disk to be formatted and press Enter.

7. In one to two minutes, you will see the message Format complete and a status report of the formatted disk. DOS then asks if you want to format another disk.

8. If you selected the /V switch, you will be asked to enter the volume label, a name of 11 characters or fewer. Type the volume label and press Enter.

9. Press Y and repeat Steps 6 through 9 to format another disk. Or, press N.

MKDIR or MD

$*$	Internal

Use MKDIR To:

Create subdirectories to help organize your file structure.

Command Syntax

MKDIR directory specifier

or

MD directory specifier

Follow These Steps

1. Type MKDIR and press the space bar.
2. You can also type the drive name and path of the new directory.
3. Type the directory name.
4. Press Enter.

MORE

 External

Use MORE To:

Display data one screen at a time. Video output pauses between pages, and the message —More— is displayed. Press any key to display the next 23 lines of data.

Command Syntax

d:path\filename.ext | MORE

Depending on your intended use of MORE, you may need to precede the syntax with a program name that will act on the file name. For example, TYPE filename.ext | MORE.

Follow These Steps

1. Type the name of the file you want displayed in groups of 23 lines and press the space bar.
2. Type the pipe symbol (|) and press the space bar.
3. Type MORE and press Enter.
4. Press any key to see more text displayed.

PATH

| $*$ | Internal |

Use PATH To:

> Access files not in the default directory, without changing directories. PATH tells DOS to search specified directories on specified drives if a program or batch file is not found in the current directory.

Command Syntax

PATH d1:\path1;d2:\path2;d3:\path3;. . .

Follow These Steps

1. Type PATH and press the space bar.
2. Type the optional drive name to be specified in the search path—for example, A:, B:, or C:. If you include the drive name with the path, DOS will find your files even if you change default drives.
3. Type the directory path to be searched—for example \KEEP.
4. Then type:

   A semi-colon if you are going to add another directory to the search path.

   The drive name and path of the additional directory to be specified in the search path.
5. Repeat Step 4 until you have completed typing all the subdirectory paths you want DOS to search.
6. Press Enter.

257

PROMPT

Use PROMPT To:

> Customize the DOS system prompt.
>
> Display the drive and directory path.
>
> Display a message on the computer.
>
> Display the date and time or the DOS version number.

Command Syntax

PROMPT promptstring

Follow These Steps

1. Type PROMPT and press the space bar.
2. Type the text string and arrangement of parameters you want.
3. You can use the meta-string characters, preceded by the dollar sign ($) with the PROMPT command to produce your own DOS prompt:

Meta-string Characters

D	the current date
G	the > character
L	the < character
N	the current disk drive name
P	the current drive and path
Q	the = character
T	the system time
V	the DOS version
Any Other	the character is ignored

REN

$$\boxed{*}\ \boxed{\text{Internal}}$$

Use RENAME To:

Change the name of a file or group of files.

Command Syntax

RENAME d:path\filename.ext filename.ext

Follow These Steps

1. Type RENAME or REN and press the space bar.
2. Type the optional drive name and path of the file to be renamed.
3. Type the file name of the file to be renamed. Wild-card characters (* and ?) may be used to specify groups of files.
4. Press the space bar.
5. Type the new name you want assigned to the file and press Enter.

RESTORE

 | External

Use RESTORE To:

Retrieve one or more files from a backup disk and store on another disk, usually a hard disk.

Command Syntax

RESTORE *sd: dd:\dpath\dfilename.ext /switches*

Follow These Steps

1. Type RESTORE and press the space bar.
2. Type the name of the source drive that contains the backed up files. For example, type **A:** to restore files from drive A. Press the space bar.
3. You can type the name of the destination drive to receive the backup files. For example, if you are restoring files to a hard disk in drive C, type C: If you omit the drive name, the default drive becomes the destination drive.
4. Type the path (directory name) if you are going to restore files from only one directory.
5. Type the name and extension of the file or files you want to restore. You can use wild-card characters to designate a group of files. For example, type *.* to designate restoration of all files on a disk or subdirectory.

Command
Reference

Installing
DOS

Common MS-DOS
Error Messages

6. Specify optional switches:

/S restores all files in the current directory and subdirectories of the current directory, creating subdirectories when necessary.

/P elicits a screen prompt that asks whether you want to restore files that have changed since the last backup or that are designated by the ATTRIB command as read-only.

/M restores only files modified or deleted since the last backup.

/N restores only files that no longer exist on the target disk.

/B:mm-dd-yy restores only those files modified on, or before, a specified date.

/A:mm-dd-yy restores only those files modified on, or after, a specified date.

/L:hh:mm:ss restores files that have changed at, or later than, a specified time.

/E:hh:mm:ss restores files that have changed at, or earlier than, a specified time.

7. Press Enter. At the prompt, place a backup disk into the source drive and press Enter once more.

8. Repeat Step 7 until all the backup disks have been processed.

261

RMDIR or RD

Use RMDIR To:

Remove a directory.

Command Syntax

RMDIR d:path

or

RD d:path

Follow These Steps

1. Use the ERASE command to delete any files from the directory to be removed. A directory must be empty to be removed. Only the current (.) and parent (..) files may remain·in the directory.
2. Type RMDIR or RD and press the space bar.
3. Type the optional drive name of the directory to be removed.
4. Type the full path and name of the subdirectory to be removed.
5. Press Enter.

SORT

 External

Use SORT To:

Read input data, sort it, and write it to an output device.

Sort and list directory information.

Display, arrange, and sort data alphabetically in ascending or descending order.

Command Syntax

\SORT /R /+n

Follow These Steps

1. Type SORT and press the space bar.
2. Specify optional switches:

    /R sorts in reverse alphabetical order.

    /+ followed by an integer representing a column number sorts in alphabetical order, starting at the specified column.

3. Press Enter.

Example:

SORT /R <PRESORT.TXT >POSTSORT.TXT

SORT will take sort, in reverse alphabetical order, the contents of the PRESORT.TXT. The sorted contents will be written to the file POSTSORT.TXT.

SYS

 External

Use SYS To:

Transfer the operating-system files to another disk. SYS is intended to permit the transfer of operating-system files to a disk that holds an applications program if there is space for the additional files.

Follow These Steps

1. Place the target disk (the disk to receive the operating system) in a disk drive.
2. Type SYS.
3. Press the space bar.
4. Type the name of the target drive that holds the disk to receive the operating system, for example, B:.
5. Press Enter. SYS will transfer the operating system to the floppy disk in the target drive.
6. If you want to make a bootable system disk, follow the SYS command with the COPY command. If your system disk is in drive A, and your target disk is in drive B, type

   COPY A:COMMAND.COM B:

TIME

Use TIME To:

Enter or change the time used by the system.

Set the automatic clock on Personal Computer ATs and PS/2 computers (beginning with DOS V3.3).

Establish the time files were newly created or modified.

Provide control for programs that require time information such as BACKUP and RESTORE.

Command Syntax

TIME hh:mm:ss.xx

Follow These Steps

1. Type TIME and press the space bar.
2. Enter the time in the format hh:mm:ss. For hh, type the hour, using one or two digits ranging from 0 to 23 hours. For mm, type the number of minutes in one or two digits ranging from 0 to 59. For ss, type the number of seconds in one or two digits ranging from 0 to 59.
3. To show hundredths of a second, you can press the period (.) and enter one to two digits from 0 to 99.
4. Press Enter.

Command Reference

TREE

 External

Use TREE To:

Display directory paths in hierarchical directories.
Optionally list the available files in each directory.
Find lost files within a maze of directories.

Command Syntax

TREE d: /F

Follow These Steps

1. Type TREE and press the space bar.
2. Type the name of the drive whose directory paths are to be displayed. The TREE command will list information pertaining to this drive.
3. You may include the following switch:
   /F lists the files in each directory.
4. Press Enter.

TYPE

| ✳ | Internal |

Use TYPE To:

Display the contents of a text file on the screen.
Send files to the printer.

Command Syntax

TYPE d:path\filename.ext

Follow These Steps

1. Type TYPE and press the space bar.
2. Type the optional drive name, path, and file name of the file to be displayed.
3. Press Enter.

Note: Use the redirection symbol > to send the typed output to a device, such as the printer (PRN).

Example:

TYPE TEXT.TXT > PRN

VER

Use VER To:

> Display the DOS version number.

Command Syntax

> VER

Follow These Steps

1. Type VER
2. Press Enter. The version number will appear on the screen along with a message like this one:

   ```
   IBM Personal Computer DOS Version 4.0
   ```

VERIFY

 Internal

Use VERIFY To:

Set your computer to check the accuracy of data written to a disk.
Show whether the data has been checked.

Command Syntax

To show whether VERIFY is on or off, use

VERIFY

To set the verify status, use

VERIFY ON

or

VERIFY OFF

Follow These Steps

1 Type VERIFY and press the space bar.
2 Type ON or OFF depending on whether you want VERIFY on to check for accuracy or off for faster disk writing operations.

VOL

Use VOL To:

Display the volume label of the specified drive.

Command Syntax

VOL d:

Follow These Steps

1. Type VOL and press the space bar.
2. Before you press Enter, you may type the drive name of the disk whose volume name you want to examine (for example, A:, B:, etc.) if that disk is not in the current drive.
3. Press Enter.

**Command
Reference**   Installing
DOS   Common MS-DOS
Error Messages

271

Appendix B

Use the disks that come in the DOS package to make a working copy of DOS. You will use the working copy with your computer, and you should store the original DOS disks in a safe place.

Before you insert any of the disks that came in your DOS package into a drive, insure that the disk is write protected. 5 1/4-inch floppy disks must have their write-protect notches covered by an adhesive, opaque tab. (In some cases, the write-protect notch on 5 1/4-inch disks is not cut and, therefore, the disk is permanently write protected.) 3 1/2-inch floppies have a write-protect window with a sliding shutter that must be open for the disk to be write-protected.

There are several versions of DOS, and various vendors of computers use specific instructions that pertain only to their versions of DOS. Check your DOS manual for instructions that may apply to your version of DOS. The general instructions in this appendix allow you to make a working copy of DOS on a floppy disk for use with this book. Remember to use the disks that came in your package only to create working copies of your original disks.

Installing MS-DOS Versions 3.3 and Earlier

Versions of DOS up to V3.3 usually contain a DOS system disk and a supplemental files or diagnostics disk. You will need the DOS system disk for this operation. To make a bootable working disk you will do the following:

1. Boot your computer using the DOS system disk.
2. Copy the DOS system disk to a new floppy disk.
3. Label the new floppy disk.

Command
Reference

**Installing
DOS**

Common MS-DOS
Error Messages

Booting with the DOS System Disk

Locate your DOS system disk and insert it into drive A. Turn the
computer on. If it is already on, press and hold down the Ctrl and Alt
keys and press the Del key. Your computer will boot from the DOS
disk. Booting will take from a few seconds to a couple of minutes.
When your computer beeps and displays screen information, read the
display. If the message NON SYSTEM DISK or an equivalent message
appears, you have chosen the wrong disk from your DOS package.
Repeat this procedure with the correct disk. If you are prompted for
the date and time, enter the current date and time. When the computer
displays the DOS prompt (almost always A>), your system is
successfully booted.

Copying the DOS System Disk

The disk-copying operation makes a working copy of your system
disk. If your package has a system disk 1 and a system disk 2, you will
need to repeat this operation to copy both disks. You can optionally
repeat this operation to make a working copy of the DOS
supplemental or diagnostics disk or other disks from your package. In
all cases **insure that the DOS package disks are write protected.**

From the keyboard, type **DISKCOPY** and be sure to press Enter. DOS
will prompt you to insert a disk or disks. Follow the sequence DOS
leads you through. When DOS refers to the *source* disk, you will insert
the DOS system disk from your DOS package into the drive specified.
When DOS refers to the *target* disk, insert the blank disk into the drive
DOS specifies. Depending on your system's memory and the number
of drives you have, the DOS messages to insert disks will vary.
Because the DOS system disk is write-protected, you will be safe from
accidental insertion of the wrong disk. When the disk copy operation
for the disk is complete, DOS will ask if you want to make another

copy. Answer **Y** for yes if you want to copy the other disks in the DOS package. Answer **N** for no if you have just one system disk to copy. When you have finished copying the disk(s) and answer N to the prompt, DOS redisplays the A> prompt.

Labeling the Copies

Remove all disks from the drives. Place a label on the DOS working disk, being careful not to touch the disk's internal surface. To write on a disk's label, use a felt-tipped pen, not a ball point pen or a pencil. If you must use a ball point pen, write on the label *before* putting it on the disk. Put the disk back into its jacket if it is a 5 1/4-inch disk. Put the original DOS disks back in their holders for safe storage away from heat, moisture, and electrical fields.

Label the copy of the system disk "DOS Working Master." If you made additional disks from your package, label them now using the "Working" description along with the name on the original disk. Since you will use the working DOS disk to learn DOS commands, there is a chance that you could erase the disk. For additional safety, you should write-protect the working copy now.

To test the working DOS disk, insert it into drive A and press Ctrl, Alt, and Del together to warm boot your system. The computer will display the DOS prompt again, and you can proceed with the exercises in this book.

Installing PC DOS V4.0

PC DOS V4.0 for IBM systems comes with an installation program called SELECT. The SELECT program can configure the DOS Shell to suit your computer's configuration. SELECT allows you to install PC DOS V4.0 on floppy disks or on a hard disk. The following procedure

Command
Reference

**Installing
DOS**

Common MS-DOS
Error Messages

shows you how to create working copies of DOS V4.0 on floppy disks. You can then use the working copies with examples in this book.

Note that PC DOS V4.0 is an operating system for IBM computers and may not work satisfactorily on other computers.

Memory Requirements for DOS V4.0 Installation

To install PC DOS V4.0, your computer must have at least 256K of random-access memory (RAM). If your system has less, ask your dealer about options to upgrade your memory. DOS V4.0's DOS Shell can be fully installed if you have at least 360K of RAM.

Floppy Disk Installation

If you are installing DOS V4.0 on 5 1/4-inch disks you will need the five 5 1/4-inch 360K disks that came with your DOS V4.0 package and four blank 5 1/4-inch 360K disks to create the working copies.

If you are installing DOS on a 3 1/2-inch 1.44M disk, you will need the two 3 1/2-inch 720K disks that came with your package and one blank 3 1/2-inch 1.44M disk to create the working copy.

If you are making the installation on a 3 1/2-inch 720K disk, you will need the two 3 1/2-inch 720K disks that came with your package and two blank 3 1/2-inch 720K disks to create the working copies.

The disks that came with the package must be write protected. For 3 1/2-inch disks, open the write-protect shutter. For 5 1/4-inch disks, cover the write-protect notch with an adhesive write-protection tab. The original 5 1/4-inch DOS disks are normally write protected permanently.

Installing DOS

Special Key Assignments for Installation

SELECT uses some of your keyboard keys for special purposes during installation. Press F1 and then F9 to see a reminder of these special key assignments. The following table summarizes the special keys in SELECT.

Table A-1
Special Key Assignments for Installation

Key	Function
Tab	Moves the cursor to the next choice.
Arrow keys	Move the cursor in the direction of the arrow key.
Enter	Takes you to the next step. (Be sure to read information presented by SELECT first.)
Esc	Takes you back to the preceding SELECT screen. Information typed on the current screen is not saved.
PgUp PgDn	Move through HELP information when it is displayed.
F1	Brings help information to the screen. During certain operations, Help is not available.
F3	Discontinues the installation process.
F9	Shows special key assignments when you view Help.

Running SELECT

If you are installing DOS V4.0 onto 360K floppies, label the four blank disks "Startup," "Shell," "Working 1", and "Working 2." If you are installing onto 720K floppies, label the two blank disks "Startup" and "Shell." If you are installing onto a 1.44M floppy, label the new disk "Startup." These new disks should *not* be write protected at this time. Make sure, however, that the original disks are write protected.

Insert the DOS V4.0 INSTALL disk in drive A. Now press and hold down the Ctrl and Alt keys and then press Del. If your system's power

Command
Reference

**Installing
DOS**

Common MS-DOS
Error Messages

is off, turn the power on instead. This step will reboot your computer and start the SELECT program.

SELECT will present an opening identification screen and ask you to press Enter to continue. If, for some reason, you don't want to continue at this point, press Esc. SELECT will ask you to pick a drive where DOS is to be installed. Depending on your hardware, this drive could be A, B, or the hard disk C. For this installation, select A or B. Use the up- or down-arrow keys to highlight your selection. Then press Enter.

During SELECT's operation, you will be asked to switch disks several times. Confirm the disk's identity by checking its label before you proceed. SELECT is designed to pick options on the installation screens that correspond to your computer's configuration. You will be safe letting SELECT make its choices. Any choices will be highlighted, and you can select them by pressing Enter.

When the installation process is complete, you can remove the DOS original V4.0 disks and store them in a safe place. The Startup disk that SELECT created will be your working DOS disk. If you have a 360K floppy system, some of the DOS external commands may be found on the Working 1 and Working 2 disks.

SELECT creates two files, AUTOEXEC.400 and CONFIG.400. These files can be renamed AUTOEXEC.BAT and CONFIG.SYS at a later time. The two files tailor the way your computer starts and configures. You learn more about these files in Chapter 10.

To see what files reside on the working disks, use the DIR /W command (Chapter 4). Any working disk that shows the file COMMAND.COM can be used to start DOS from drive A. Normally, the Startup disk will serve as your working DOS disk. The Shell disk will start the DOS Shell. You can exit the Shell and go to the DOS prompt to do the exercises in this book.

Installing DOS

Hard Disk Installation

CAUTION: If you do not know how to prepare your hard disk, you could inadvertently select an installation option that would cause permanent loss of data from your hard disk. This section on hard disk installation is intended for experienced users. Please use caution.

You can optionally run the installation operation to install V4.0 onto your hard disk, but you should follow certain precautions before hard disk installation. If your computer is on a local area network (LAN), consult the network administrator before attempting to install V4.0 on your system. If you share backed up files with other computer users under the guidance of a lead user, ask the lead user to become familiar with the implications of BACKUP and RESTORE before proceeding with hard disk installation of V4.0.

If you bought your computer and DOS V4.0 from a dealer, ask the dealer to assist you with hard disk installation of DOS. If you have another operating system already installed on your hard disk, such as OS/2, XENIX, or UNIX among others, you will need to read and understand the IBM DOS V4.0 *Getting Started* manual's discussion. For hard disk installation of PC DOS 4.0, you will need one new or blank floppy disk, which SELECT will use to record your configuration options during the installation.

If you are familiar with the DOS FDISK command and understand the implications of preparing a hard disk, you can follow the procedures for installing DOS 4.0 to a hard disk. If you do not know about FDISK, do not select hard disk installation from SELECT's options. SELECT does not require you to run FDISK, but SELECT does prompt you for selections which are based on the functions of FDISK.

Command
Reference

**Installing
DOS**

Common MS-DOS
Error Messages

SELECT optionally installs DOS 4.0 to your hard disk if a hard disk is detected. SELECT allows you to automatically partition your hard disk if it does not have a primary DOS partition. SELECT then formats the hard disk after it has done the partitioning step. Hard disks that are already partitioned prior to running SELECT are not partitioned again by SELECT if you allow SELECT to make its own choices at the prompts. If you have a new hard disk which has no partition on it, SELECT will volunteer this step as part of the installation process.

If your hard disk has already been partitioned and formatted, SELECT will copy the hidden system files to your hard disk from the DOS V4.0 disk. You can optionally specify a directory to hold the DOS V4.0 commands and utilities. By default, SELECT copies the commands and utilities as well as the Shell files to the \DOS directory. Any command or utility files with duplicate names in the directory you choose will be replaced during V4.0 installation.

SELECT detects hard disks that only need upgrading of the DOS version to 4.0. Except for changing the DOS files, SELECT leaves the existing file system intact if no partitioning or formatting of the hard disk is required.

Since DOS V4.0 supports partitions larger than 32M, users who have hard disks with capacities greater than 32M may elect to remove existing partitions and install one large partition to take advantage of V4.0's larger partition size capability. Remember that removing a partition will destroy the files in that partition.

The booklet, *Getting Started,* that comes in the PC DOS V4.0 package devotes many sections to hard disk installation. You should consider that booklet the source for additional information about installing PC DOS V4.0.

Appendix C

The actual wordings of common error messages differ for different implementations and versions of MS-DOS. Sometimes the differences may be as slight as punctuation and capitalization. At other times, the entire content of the message may differ. If you see a message that you cannot locate in this guide, refer to your computer's MS-DOS manual.

The messages may appear when you are starting MS-DOS or when you are using your computer. Most start-up errors mean that MS-DOS did not start and that you must reboot the system. Most of the other error messages mean that MS-DOS terminated (aborted) the program and returned to the system prompt. The messages are listed in alphabetical order for easy reference.

Bad command or filename

The name you entered is not valid for invoking a command, program, or batch file. The most frequent causes are the following: (1) you misspelled a name; (2) you omitted a needed disk drive or path name; or (3) you gave the parameters without the command name.

Check the spelling on the command line. Make sure that the command, program, or batch file is in the location specified (disk drive and directory path). Then try the command again.

Bad or missing Command Interpreter

MS-DOS cannot find the command interpreter, COMMAND.COM. MS-DOS does not start.

Command
Reference

Installing
DOS

**Common MS-DOS
Error Messages**

If you are starting MS-DOS, this message means that COMMAND.COM is not on the boot disk or that a version of COMMAND.COM from a previous version of MS-DOS is on the disk. Place in the floppy disk drive another disk that contains the operating system and then reboot the system. After MS-DOS has started, copy COMMAND.COM to the original start-up disk so that you can boot from that disk.

If this message appears while you are running MS-DOS, the reason may be that COMMAND.COM has been erased from the disk and directory you used when starting MS-DOS or that a version of COMMAND.COM from a previous MS-DOS has overwritten the good version. You must restart MS-DOS by resetting the system.

If resetting the system does not solve your problem, use a copy of your MS-DOS master disk to restart the computer. Copy COMMAND.COM from this floppy disk to the offending disk.

Bad or missing filename

MS-DOS was directed to load a device driver that could not be located, an error occurred when the device driver was loaded, or a break address for the device driver was out of bounds for the size of RAM memory being used in the computer. MS-DOS will continue its boot but will not use the device driver filename.

If MS-DOS loads, check your CONFIG.SYS file for the line DEVICE=filename. Make sure that the line is spelled correctly and that the device driver is where you specified. If this line is correct, reboot the system. If the message appears again, copy the file from its original disk to the boot disk and try booting MS-DOS again. If the error persists, contact the dealer who sold you the driver, because the device driver is bad.

281

Common MS-DOS Error Messages

`Batch file missing`

MS-DOS could not find the batch file it was processing. The batch file may have been erased or renamed. For MS-DOS V3.0 only, the disk containing the batch file may have been changed. MS-DOS aborts the processing of the batch file.

If you are using MS-DOS V3.0 and you changed the floppy disk that contains the batch file, restart the batch file and do not change the disk. You may need to edit the batch file so that you will not need to change disks.

If you renamed the batch file, rename it again, using the original name. If required, edit the batch file to ensure that the file name does not get changed again.

If the file was erased, re-create the batch file from its backup file if possible. Edit the file to ensure that the batch file does not erase itself.

`Cannot load COMMAND.COM, system halted`

MS-DOS attempted to reload COMMAND.COM, but the area where MS-DOS keeps track of available and used memory was destroyed, or the command processor was not found. The system halts.

This message may indicate that COMMAND.COM has been erased from the disk and directory you used when starting MS-DOS. Restart MS-DOS. If it does not start, the copy of COMMAND.COM has been erased. Restart MS-DOS from the original master disks and copy COMMAND.COM to your working disk.

Another possible cause for this message is that an erroneous program corrupted the memory allocation table where MS-DOS tracks available memory. Reboot and then try running the same program that was in the computer when the system halted. If the problem occurs again, the program is defective. Contact the dealer who sold you the program.

Cannot start COMMAND.COM, exiting

MS-DOS was directed to load an additional copy of COMMAND.COM, but could not. Either your CONFIG.SYS FILES= command is set too low, or you do not have enough free memory for another copy of COMMAND.COM.

If your system has 256K or more and FILES is less than 10, edit the CONFIG.SYS file on your start-up disk and use FILES = 15 or FILES = 20; then reboot.

If the problem occurs again, you do not have enough memory in your computer or you have too many programs competing for memory space. Restart MS-DOS again and do not load any resident or background programs you do not need. If necessary, eliminate unneeded device drivers or RAM-disk software. Another alternative is to increase the amount of random-access memory in your system.

Configuration too large

MS-DOS could not load itself because you specified too many FILES or BUFFERS in your CONFIG.SYS file.

Common MS-DOS Error Messages

Restart MS-DOS with a different disk and edit the CONFIG.SYS file on your boot disk, lowering the number of FILES and/or BUFFERS. Restart MS-DOS with the edited disk. Another alternative is to increase the RAM memory in your system.

Current drive is no longer valid

You have set the system prompt to PROMPT $p. At the system level, MS-DOS attempted to read the current directory for the disk drive and found the drive no longer valid.

If the current disk drive is set for a floppy disk, this warning appears when you do not have a disk in the disk drive. MS-DOS reports a `Drive not ready` error. You give the **F** command to fail (which is the same as A for abort) or the **I** command to ignore the error. Then insert a floppy disk into the disk drive.

The invalid drive error also can happen if you have a networked disk drive that has been deleted or disconnected. Simply change the current disk to a valid disk drive.

Disk boot failure

An error occurred when MS-DOS tried to load itself into memory. The disk contained IO.SYS and MSDOS.SYS, but one of the two files could not be loaded. MS-DOS did not boot.

Try starting MS-DOS from the disk again. If the error recurs, try booting MS-DOS from a disk you know is good, such as a copy of your MS-DOS master disk. If this action fails, you have a hardware disk drive problem. Contact your local dealer.

Drive not ready

An error occurred while MS-DOS tried to read or write to the disk drive. For floppy disk drives, the drive door may be open, the disk may not be inserted, or the disk may not be formatted. For hard disk drives, the drive may not be properly prepared or you may have a hardware problem.

Error in EXE file

MS-DOS detected an error while attempting to load a program stored in an EXE file. The problem is in the relocation information MS-DOS needs to load the program. This problem can occur if the .EXE file has been altered in any way.

Restart MS-DOS and try the program again, this time using a backup copy of the program. If the message reappears, the program is flawed. If you are using a purchased program, contact the dealer or publisher.

Error loading operating system

A disk error occurred while MS-DOS was loading itself from the hard disk. MS-DOS does not boot.

Restart the computer. If the error occurs after several tries, restart MS-DOS from the floppy disk drive. If the hard disk does not respond (that is, if you cannot run DIR or CHKDSK without getting an error message), you have a problem with the hard disk. Contact your local dealer. If the hard disk does respond, use the SYS command to put another copy of MS-DOS onto your hard disk. You may need to copy COMMAND.COM to the hard disk also.

Common MS-DOS Error Messages

EXEC failure

MS-DOS encountered an error while reading a command or program from the disk, or the CONFIG.SYS FILES= command has too low a value.

Increase the number of FILES in the CONFIG.SYS file of your start-up disk to 15 or 20 and then restart MS-DOS. If the error recurs, you may have a problem with the disk. Use a backup copy of the program and try again. If the backup copy works, copy it over the offending copy.

If an error occurs in the copying process, you have a flawed floppy disk or hard disk. If the problem is a floppy disk, copy the files from the flawed disk to another disk and reformat or retire the original floppy disk. If the problem is the hard disk, immediately back up your files and get assistance in running RECOVER on the offending file. If the problem persists, your hard disk may have a hardware failure.

File creation error

A program or MS-DOS attempted to add a new file to the directory or replace an existing file, but failed.

If the file already exists, it may be a read-only file. If the problem is not a read-only file, run CHKDSK without the /F switch to determine whether the directory is full, the disk is full, or some other problem exists with the disk.

File not found

MS-DOS could not find the file you specified. The file is not on the disk or directory you specified or you misspelled the disk drive name,

Command
Reference

Installing
DOS

**Common MS-DOS
Error Messages**

path name, or file name. Check these possibilities and try the
command again.

General failure

This is a catchall error message. The error usually occurs when you
use an unformatted floppy disk or hard disk, or when you leave the
disk drive door open.

Incorrect MS-DOS version

The copy of the file holding the command you just entered is from a
different version of MS-DOS.

Get a copy of the command from the correct version of MS-DOS
(usually from your copy of the MS-DOS master disk) and try the
command again. If the floppy disk or hard disk you are using has been
updated to hold new versions of the MS-DOS programs, copy those
versions over the old ones.

Insert disk with \COMMAND.COM in drive d and strike any key when ready

MS-DOS needs to reload COMMAND.COM but can not find it on the
start-up disk.

If you are using floppy disks, probably the disk in drive A has been
changed. Place a disk holding a good copy of COMMAND.COM in
drive A: and press a key.

Common MS-DOS Error Messages

```
Insert disk with batch file
and strike any key when ready
```

MS-DOS is attempting to execute the next command from a batch file, but the disk holding the batch file was removed from the disk drive. This message occurs for MS-DOS V3.1. MS-DOS V3.0 gives an error message when the disk is changed.

Put the disk holding the batch file into the disk drive and press a key to continue.

```
Insufficient disk space
```

The disk does not have enough free space to hold the file being written. All MS-DOS programs terminate when this problem occurs, but some non-DOS programs continue.

If you think that the disk has enough room to hold this file, run CHKDSK to see whether the floppy disk or hard disk has a problem. Sometimes when you terminate programs early by pressing Ctrl-Break, MS-DOS is not allowed to do the necessary clean-up work. When this happens, disk space is temporarily trapped. CHKDSK can "free" these areas.

If you simply have run out of disk space, free some disk space or use a different floppy disk or hard disk. Try the command again.

```
Insufficient memory
```

The computer does not have enough free RAM to execute the program or command.

If you loaded a RAM-resident program like SideKick or ProKey, restart MS-DOS and try the command before loading any resident program. If this method fails, remove any unneeded device driver or RAM-disk software from the CONFIG.SYS file and restart MS-DOS again. If this action fails, your computer does not have enough memory for this command. You must increase your random-access memory to run the command.

Invalid COMMAND.COM in drive d

MS-DOS tried to reload COMMAND.COM from the disk in drive d and found that the file was of a different version of MS-DOS. You will see a message instructing you to insert a disk with the correct version and press a key. Follow the directions for that message.

If you frequently use the disk that was originally in the disk drive, copy the correct version of COMMAND.COM to that disk.

Invalid COMMAND.COM, system halted

MS-DOS could not find COMMAND.COM on the hard disk. MS-DOS halts and must be restarted.

COMMAND.COM may have been erased. Restart the computer from the hard disk. If you see a message indicating that COMMAND.COM is missing, that file was erased. Restart MS-DOS from a floppy disk and recopy COMMAND.COM to the root directory of the hard disk.

If you restart MS-DOS and this message appears later, a program or batch file may be erasing COMMAND.COM. If a batch file is erasing

Common MS-DOS Error Messages

COMMAND.COM, edit the batch file. If a program is erasing
COMMAND.COM, contact the dealer who sold you the program.

Invalid directory

One of the following errors occurred: (1) you specified a directory
name that does not exist; (2) you misspelled the directory name; (3)
the directory path is on a different disk; (4) you forgot to give the path
character (\) at the beginning of the name; or (5) you did not separate
the directory names with the path character. Check your directory
names, ensure that the directories do exist, and try the command
again.

Invalid disk change

The disk in the 720K, 1.2M, or 1.44M disk drive was changed while a
program had open files to be written to the disk. You will see the
message `Abort, Retry, Fail`. Place the correct disk in the disk
drive and type **R** for Retry.

Invalid drive in search path

One specification you gave to the PATH command has an invalid disk
drive name, or a named disk drive is nonexistent.

Use PATH to check the paths you instructed MS-DOS to search. If you
gave a nonexistent disk drive name, use the PATH command again
and enter the correct search paths. Or you can just ignore the warning
message.

Invalid drive specification

This message is given when one of the following errors occurs: (1) you
have entered the name of an invalid or nonexistent disk drive as a
parameter to a command; (2) you have given the same disk drive for
the source and destination, which is not permitted for the command;
or (3) by not giving a parameter, you have defaulted to the same
source and destination disk drive.

Certain MS-DOS commands temporarily hide disk drive names while
the command is in effect. Check the disk drive names. If the command
is objecting to a missing parameter and defaulting to the wrong disk
drive, explicitly name the correct disk drive.

Invalid drive specification
Specified drive does not exist,
or is non-removable

One of the following errors occurred: (1) you gave the name of a
nonexistent disk drive; (2) you named the hard disk drive when using
commands for floppy disks only; (3) you did not give a disk drive
name and defaulted to the hard disk when using commands for floppy
disks only; or (4) you named or defaulted to a RAM-disk drive when
using commands for a "real" floppy disk only.

Remember that certain MS-DOS commands temporarily hide disk drive
names while the command is in effect. Check the disk drive name you
gave and try the command again.

Common MS-DOS Error Messages

`Invalid number of parameters`

You have given either too few or too many parameters to a command. One of the following errors occurred: (1) you omitted required information; (2) you forgot a colon immediately after the disk drive name; (3) you put a space in the wrong place or omitted a needed space; or (4) you forgot to place a slash (/) in front of a switch.

`Invalid parameter`
`Incorrect parameter`

At least one parameter you entered for the command is not valid. One of the following occurred: (1) you omitted required information; (2) you forgot a colon immediately after the disk drive name; (3) you put a space in the wrong place or omitted a needed space; (4) you forgot to place a slash (/) in front of a switch; or (5) you used a switch the command does not recognize.

Also check this message under the individual command for more information.

`Invalid path`

One of the following errors has occurred to a path name you have entered: (1) the path name contains illegal characters; (2) the name has more than 63 characters; or (3) one of the directory names within the path is misspelled or does not exist.

Check the spelling of the path name. If needed, do a DIR of the disk and ensure that the directory you have specified does exist and that you have the correct path name. Be sure that the path name contains 63 characters or fewer. If necessary, change the current directory to a directory "closer" to the file and shorten the path name.

Lock violation

With the file-sharing program (SHARE.EXE) or network software loaded, one of your programs attempted to access a file that is locked. Your best choice is **R**etry. Then try **A**bort or **F**ail. If you choose abort or fail, however, any data in memory is lost.

Memory allocation error
Cannot load COMMAND, system halted

A program destroyed the area where MS-DOS keeps track of in-use and available memory. You must restart MS-DOS.

If this error occurs again with the same program, the program has a flaw. Use a backup copy of the program. If the problem persists, contact the dealer or program publisher.

Missing operating system

The MS-DOS hard disk partition does not have a copy of MS-DOS on it. MS-DOS does not boot.

Start MS-DOS from a floppy disk. If you have existing files on the hard disk, back up the files. Issue **FORMAT /S** to put a copy of the operating system on the hard disk. If necessary, restore the files that you backed up.

Non-System disk or disk error
Replace and strike any key when ready

Your floppy disk or hard disk does not contain MS-DOS, or a read error occurred when you started the system. MS-DOS does not boot.

293

If you are using a floppy disk system, put a bootable disk in drive A and press a key.

The most frequent cause of this message on hard disk systems is that you left a nonbootable floppy disk in disk drive A with the door closed. Open the door to disk drive A and press a key. MS-DOS will boot from the hard disk.

`No paper`

The printer is either out of paper or is not turned on.

`Non-DOS disk`

The disk is unusable. You can abort and run CHKDSK on the disk to see whether any corrective action is possible. If CHKDSK fails, your other alternative is to reformat the disk. Reformatting, however, will destroy any remaining information on the disk. If you use more than one operating system, the disk was probably formatted under the operating system you're using and should not be reformatted.

`Not enough memory`

The computer does not have enough free random-access memory to execute the program or command.

If you loaded a RAM-resident program like SideKick or ProKey, restart MS-DOS and try the command again before loading any resident program. If this method fails, remove any unneeded device driver or RAM-disk software from the CONFIG.SYS file and restart MS-DOS again. If this option fails also, your computer does not have enough memory for this command. You must increase your RAM to run the command.

Command
Reference

Installing
DOS

**Common MS-DOS
Error Messages**

Not ready

A device is not ready and cannot receive or transmit data. Check the connections, make sure that the power is on, and check to see whether the device is ready.

Path not found

A file or directory path you named does not exist. You may have misspelled the file name or directory name, or you omitted a path character (\) between directory names or between the final directory name and file name. Another possibility is that the file or directory does not exist where you specified. Check these possibilities and try again.

Path too long

You have given a path name that exceeds the 63 character limit of MS-DOS. Either the name is too long, or you omitted a space between file names. Check the command line. If the phrasing is correct, you must change to a directory that is closer to the file you want and try the command again.

Program too big to fit in memory

The computer does not have enough memory to load the program or command you invoked.

If you have any resident programs loaded (such as SideKick), restart MS-DOS and try the command again without loading the resident programs. If this message appears again, reduce the number of buffers (BUFFERS=) in the CONFIG.SYS file, eliminate unneeded device

Common MS-DOS Error Messages

drivers or RAM-disk software, and restart MS-DOS. If these actions do not solve the problem, your computer does not have enough memory for the program or command. You must increase the amount of RAM in your computer to run this command.

Read fault

MS-DOS was unable to read the data, usually from a hard disk or floppy disk. Check the disk drive doors and be sure that the disk is properly inserted.

Sector not found

The disk drive was unable to locate the sector on the floppy disk or hard disk platter. This error is usually the result of a defective spot on the disk or of defective drive electronics. Some copy-protection schemes also use this method (a defective spot) to prevent unauthorized duplication of the disk.

Seek

The disk drive could not locate the proper track on the floppy disk or hard disk platter. This error is usually the result of a defective spot on the floppy disk or hard disk platter, an unformatted disk, or drive electronics problems.

Syntax error

You phrased a command improperly by (1) omitting needed information; (2) giving extraneous information; (3) putting an extra space in a file name or path name; or (4) using an incorrect switch. Check the command line for these possibilities and try the command again.

Command
Reference

Installing
DOS

**Common MS-DOS
Error Messages**

Unable to create directory

Either you or a program has attempted to create a directory, and one of the following has occurred: (1) a directory by the same name already exists; (2) a file by the same name already exists; (3) you are adding a directory to the root directory, and the root directory is full; or (4) the directory name has illegal characters or is a device name.

Do a DIR of the disk. Make sure that no file or directory already exists with the same name. If you are adding the directory to the root directory, remove or move (copy, then erase) any unneeded files or directives. Check the spelling of the directory and ensure that the command is properly phrased.

Unrecognized command in CONFIG.SYS

MS-DOS detected an improperly phrased directive in CONFIG.SYS. The directive is ignored, and MS-DOS continues to start; but MS-DOS does not indicate the incorrect line. Examine the CONFIG.SYS file, looking for improperly phrased or incorrect directives. Edit the line, save the file, and restart MS-DOS.

Write fault

MS-DOS could not write the data to this device. Perhaps you inserted the floppy disk improperly, or you left the disk drive door open. Another possibility is an electronics failure in the floppy or hard disk drive. The most frequent cause is a bad spot on the disk.

Write protect

The disk is write-protected.

297

Index

.BAK file extension, 152-153

.BAS file extension, 43

.BAT file extension, 43

Batch file missing message, 281

batch files, 41, 206-231

    creating with word processing programs, 211

    rules for, 208-209

    running, 50

binary digits, 36

BIOS, 41

bits, 9, 36

boot-strap loader, 54

buffers, 85, 224-225, 229

BUFFERS directive, 225, 229

buses, 37, 39

bytes, 9, 36

bytes in bad sector message, 111

C

/C switch, FIND command, 251

calendar, setting, 50

Cannot load COMMAND.COM, system halted message, 281

Cannot start COMMAND.COM, exiting message, 283

CD command, 131, 134-135, 153, 236

characters

    backslash (\), 122-125

    meta-string, 216, 258

    wild card, 90-91, 95

CHDIR command, 131, 134-135, 153, 236

CHKDSK (Check Disk) command, 201-205, 237-238

    /F switch, 238

    /V switch, 202, 238

    with BACKUP command, 202-203

Clear Screen command, 200, 239

clock, setting, 50

.CLR file extension, 43\

CLS (Clear Screen) command, 200, 239

codes, extended ASCII, 15

cold boot, 56-60

color graphics adapter (CGA), 14

.COM file extensions, 42

command

    file, 42, 213-214

    interpreter, 44

    line editing keys, 85

    rule of currents, 233

    syntax, 76, 78-79, 82

COMMAND.COM file 44, 47, 50, 84, 103, 107, 126, 132-133, 206, 277, 281-283, 289-290

commands

    CD, 131, 134-135, 153, 236

    RD, 131-132

    adding parameters, 84-86

    BACKUP, 172-173, 178-187, 234-235

Introduction

Personal Computers

Disk Operating Systems

Booting the Computer

Using DOS Commands

Preparing Disks

Hierarchical Directories

Copying and Deleting Files

Protecting Data

Special Commands

Batch Files

Appendix A

Appendix B

Appendix C

Index

Index

D

Introduction

Personal
Computers

Disk
Operating
Systems

Booting the
Computer

Using DOS
Commands

Preparing
Disks

Hierarchical
Directories

Copying and
Deleting Files

Protecting
Data

Special
Commands

Batch Files

Appendix A

Appendix B

Appendix C

Index

Index

E

Introduction

Personal
Computers

Disk
Operating
Systems

Booting the
Computer

Using DOS
Commands

Preparing
Disks

Hierarchical
Directories

Copying and
Deleting Files

Protecting
Data

Special
Commands

Batch Files

Appendix A

Appendix B

Appendix C

Index

Index

single, 151-152, 160-161
to another directory, 153-154, 166-167
to same disk directory, 152-153, 164-165
deleting, 168-171
executable, 43
hidden, 44
managing, 48
renaming, 168-171
utility, 45
V4.0 AUTOEXEC.400, 212
filters, 193
FIND command, 193, 251-252
/C switch, 251
/N switch, 251
fixed disks, 28
floppy disk, 27-28, 179-181
floppy disk drive, 32-33
Format another (Y/N)? message, 111
FORMAT command, 96-106, 183, 201, 253-254
/1 switch, 103, 253
/4 switch, 103, 253
/8 switch, 103, 253
/B switch, 254
/N switch, 103, 254
/S switch, 103, 105253
/T switch, 103, 254
/V switch, 102-103, 201, 253
error messages, 110-113
formatting disks, 48, 96-102, 114-115
floppy disk drive, 99-102
hard disk drive, 102
hard disks, 114-115

fragmentation, 150, 203
function keys, 20, 22-25

G

---

games, 13
General failure message, 287
graphics, 13
adaptors, 14
display, 16
uses in book, 4

H

---

hard disk, 27-29, 114-115
backing up, 178-187
bay, 32
drive, 32-33, 178-187
formatting, 102, 114-115
platters, 33
hardware, 10,14-36, 46-47
failures, 174-177
necessary for MS-DOS, 7
hidden files, 44
hierarchial
directory commands, 130-136
directories, 116-139
directory system, 118-122

HLP file extension, 43
home finance, 13

I

Incorrect MS-DOS version message, 287
Incorrect parameter message, 292
input, 9, 36
input device, 20-25
input/output, redirecting, 49
Insert disk with batch file and strike any key when ready message, 288
Insert disk with \COMMAND COM in drive d and strike any key when ready message, 287
installation, 272-280
　　to floppy disk, 275-277
　　to hard disk, 277-279
　　V4.0, 274-279
Insufficient disk space message, 288-289
integrated programs, 13
interface, 41, 49
internal commands, 76, 109
interpreters, command, 44
Invalid COMMAND.COM in drive d message, 289
Invalid COMMAND.COM, system

halted message, 289-290
Invalid directory messages, 290
Invalid disk change message, 290
Invalid drive in search path message, 290
Invalid drive specification Specified drive does not exist or non-removable, 291
Invalid drive specification message, 291
Invalid media or track 0 bad - disk unusable message, 111
Invalid number of parameters message, 292
Invalid parameter message, 292
Invalid path message, 292
issuing, 84-88

J

joysticks, 34

K

K (kilobyte), 9
key combinations, 24

Introduction

Personal Computers

Disk Operating Systems

Booting the Computer

Using DOS Commands

Preparing Disks

Hierarchical Directories

Copying and Deleting Files

Protecting Data

Special Commands

Batch Files

Appendix A

Appendix B

Appendix C

Index

Index

keyboards, 20-25

keys,
    command line editing, 85
    Ctrl Alt Del, 75
    Ctrl Break, 75, 169, 179
    Ctrl-C, 75, 169, 179
    Ctrl-S, 88
    Esc, 85-86
    function, 20, 22-25
    online help, 20
    Pause, 88
    Shift PrtSc, 20
    special, 22-23

L

/L switch, RESTORE command, 187, 261

labeling disks, 272

labels, volume, 102-103

laser printer, 29-31

line editing keys, 85

liquid crystal display (LCD), 14

location, within book, 2

Lock violation message, 292

logged drive, 73-74 ·

M

M (megabyte), 9

/M switch,
    BACKUP command, 183, 187, 235
    RESTORE command, 187, 261

magnetic storage, 11

math coprocessor, 32

MD command, 130, 134-135

Memory allocation error message, 292

memory disks, 111

memory, 11

messages,
    Bad command or filename, 80, 233, 279-280
    Bad or missing Command Interpreter, 280
    Bad or missing filename, 281
    Batch file missing, 282
    Bytes in bad sector, 110
    Cannot load COMMAND.COM, system halted, 282
    Cannot start COMMAND.COM, exiting, 283
    Configuration too large, 283-284
    Current drive is no longer valid, 284
    Disk boot failure, 284

Introduction

Personal
Computers

Disk
Operating
Systems

Booting the
Computer

Using DOS
Commands

Preparing
Disks

Hierarchical
Directories

Copying and
Deleting Files

Protecting
Data

Special
Commands

Batch Files

Appendix A

Appendix B

Appendix C

Index

Index

microprocessor, 8, 32

Missing operating system message, 292

mistakes, preventing, 175-177

MKDIR command, 130, 134-135, 255

mode, nondocument, 208

modems, 9, 31-32, 34

monitor, 14-19

monochrome display adapter (MDA), 14-15

MORE command, 193, 256

MOS file extension, 43

motherboard, 26, 32

mouse, 29, 34

MS-DOS
    defined, 3
    necessary hardware, 7

N

/N switch,
    FIND command, 251
    FORMAT command 103, 254
    RESTORE command, 187, 261

No paper message, 294

NON SYSTEM DISK message, 273

Non-DOS disk message, 294

nonstandard keyboard, 21, 25

Non-system disk or disk error

Replace and strike any key when ready message, 293-294

nondocument mode, 208

Not enough memory message, 294

Not ready message, 295

Not ready reading drive A Abort, Retry, Fail? message

O

---

online help key, 20

operating systems, 13

output, 9, 36
    characters, 30-31
    default, 14

P

/P switch,
    DIR command, 81, 83, 93, 244
    RESTORE command, 187, 261

parallel printers, 30

parameters, 78, 84-86

PATH command, 132-133, 138, 142, 193, 201, 214-215, 219-220, 256-257, 290

path names, 122, 124-125

Path not found message, 295

path specifier, 132

Path too long message, 295

Pause key, 88

peripherals, 9, 26, 34
    hardware, 10

picture element, 18

pipes, 193

pixels, 14

plotters, 35

point and shoot software, 29

port, 30

power on reset (POR), 57

power on self test, (POST), 57, 59

preliminary checks, 56

preparing disks, 96-115

Press any key to continue message,
    81

printers, 29-31, 35
    daisywheel, 29-31
    dot-matrix, 29-31
    laser, 29-31
    parallel, 30
    serial, 30

printing, with Shift PrtSc, 20

.PRO file extension, 43

Program too big to fit in memory
    message, 295-296

programs,13, 37, 41, 49

PROMPT command, 214-220, 258

prompt view, 60, 64

protecting data, 172-187

.PRT file extension, 43

Q

QWERTY layout, 20

R

/R switch, SORT command, 263

RAM, 32, 37, 44, 57, 224

RAM disk, 111

random access memory, 32, 37, 44,
    57, 224

RD command, 131-132, 262

Read fault message, 296

read only memory, 37, 45

read/writing, 26

redirecting input/output, 49

redirecting to printer, 192-193

redirection, 41, 190-200

redirection symbols, 191-193, 198-
    199, 216

RENAME command, 168-171, 259

renaming files, 168-171

resolution, 14, 18

RESTORE command, 114, 172-173,
    184-187, 260-261
    /A switch, 187, 261
    /B switch, 261

Introduction

Personal
Computers

Disk
Operating
Systems

Booting the
Computer

Using DOS
Commands

Preparing
Disks

Hierarchical
Directories

Copying and
Deleting Files

Protecting
Data

Special
Commands

Batch Files

Appendix A

Appendix B

Appendix C

Index

Index

Index

TREE command, 133, 139, 266
TREE command
  /F switch, 133, 266
tree structure, 118
two-state principle, 36
TYPE command, 192-193, 209, 220, 267

U

Unable to create directory message, 297
Unrecognized command in
  CONFIG.SYS message, 297
uses of DOS, 48-53
utilities, 13
utility files, 45

V

/V switch
  CHKDSK command, 202, 238
  COPY command, 148, 153, 156-163, 240-241
  FIND command, 251

FORMAT command, 102-103, 201, 253
V4.0
  AUTOEXEC.400 file, 212
  changing screen colors, 68
  commands
    MEM, 200, 204
    DOSSHELL 61-63
    Memory Report (MEM) 200, 204
  File System screen, 67-68, 71
  installation, 273-278
  MEM command, 200, 204
  Memory Report command (MEM) 200, 204
  Select program, 274-279
  selection cursor 253-404
  shell view, 60-72
  shell, leaving, 63
  shell, returning with exit, 63
  Start Programs screen, 62, 65, 70
  Start Programs screen, Main
    Group items, 66-72
  Utilities screen, 69
values, default, 106
VERIFY command, 201, 204, 269
Version command (VER), 200, 204, 268
Versions of DOS, 51
video graphics adapter (VGA), 14
virtual disks, 111
VOL command, 201, 204, 270
volume label, 89, 102-103

W

/W switch, DIR command, 81, 83, 93, 244

warm boot, Ctrl, Alt, Del keys, 72, 75

wild cards

., 149, 151, 169, 185

?, 155

characters, 90-91, 95

COPY command, 149, 151, 155

DEL command, 169

ERASE command, 169

RENAME command, 169

RESTORE command, 183

Winchester disks, 28

word-processing programs, 13

creating batch files, 211

working disks, creating, 273

Write fault message, 297

Write protect message, 297

write-protecting disks, 270

Introduction

Personal
Computers

Disk
Operating
Systems

Booting the
Computer

Using DOS
Commands

Preparing
Disks

Hierarchical
Directories

Copying and
Deleting Files

Protecting
Data

Special
Commands

Batch Files

Appendix A

Appendix B

Appendix C

Index

More Computer Knowledge from Que

For more information, call

1-800-428-5331

All prices subject to change without notice. Prices and charges are for domestic orders only. Non-U.S. prices might be higher.

SELECT QUE BOOKS TO INCREASE
YOUR PERSONAL COMPUTER PRODUCTIVITY

Using PC DOS, 3rd Edition
by Chris DeVoney

This classic text offers a complete overview of the new commands and user interface of DOS 4.0, and a useful **Command Reference** section.

Order #961
$23.95 USA
0-88022-419-3, 850 pp.

MS-DOS User's Guide, 3rd Edition
by Chris DeVoney

Updated for Version 4.0! Includes expanded EDLIN coverage and an introduction to the DOS shell. Also contains several extended tutorials, basic command syntax, and in-depth DOS data. This is a must for everyone who uses DOS!

$22.95 USA
Order #838
0-88022-349-9
756 pp.

DOS QueCards
Developed by Que Corporation

QueCards are 5" x 8" cards that show the proper use of DOS commands and functions. Covers both PC DOS and MS-DOS 3.3.

Order #828
$21.95 USA
0-88022-339-1, 100 cards/200 pages

MS-DOS Quick Reference
Developed by Que Corporation

Complete, compact reference for the essential operations of DOS 3.X and DOS 4! This easy-to-use reference provides instant access to the most commonly used DOS commands and functions. It's perfect for laptop or desktop computer users!

Order #865
7.95 USA
0-88022-369-3, 160 pp.

Free Catalog!

Mail us this registration form today, and we'll send you a free catalog featuring Que's complete line of best-selling books.

Name of Book _____

Name _____

Title _____

Phone (___) _____

Company _____

Address _____

City _____

State _____ ZIP _____

Please check the appropriate answers:

1. Where did you buy your Que book?
   - ☐ Bookstore (name: _____)
   - ☐ Computer store (name: _____)
   - ☐ Catalog (name: _____)
   - ☐ Direct from Que
   - ☐ Other: _____

2. How many computer books do you buy a year?
   - ☐ 1 or less
   - ☐ 2-5
   - ☐ 6-10
   - ☐ More than 10

3. How many Que books do you own?
   - ☐ 1
   - ☐ 2-5
   - ☐ 6-10
   - ☐ More than 10

4. How long have you been using this software?
   - ☐ Less than 6 months
   - ☐ 6 months to 1 year
   - ☐ 1-3 years
   - ☐ More than 3 years

5. What influenced your purchase of this Que book?
   - ☐ Personal recommendation
   - ☐ Advertisement
   - ☐ In-store display
   - ☐ Price
   - ☐ Que catalog
   - ☐ Que mailing
   - ☐ Que's reputation
   - ☐ Other: _____

6. How would you rate the overall content of the book?
   - ☐ Very good
   - ☐ Good
   - ☐ Satisfactory
   - ☐ Poor

7. What do you like *best* about this Que book?
   _____
   _____

8. What do you like *least* about this Que book?
   _____
   _____

9. Did you buy this book with your personal funds?
   - ☐ Yes   ☐ No

10. Please feel free to list any other comments you may have about this Que book.
    _____
    _____
    _____

— Que —

Order Your Que Books Today!

Name _____

Title _____

Company _____

City _____

State _____ ZIP _____

Phone No. (___) _____

Method of Payment:

Check ☐ (Please enclose in envelope.)

Charge My: VISA ☐   MasterCard ☐
American Express ☐

Charge # _____

Expiration Date _____

Order No.	Title	Qty.	Price	Total

You can **FAX** your order to **1-317-573-2583**. Or call **1-800-428-5331, ext. ORDR** to order direct.
Please add $2.50 per title for shipping and handling.

Subtotal _____

Shipping & Handling _____

Total _____

— Que —

BUSINESS REPLY MAIL
First Class Permit No. 9918   Indianapolis, IN

Postage will be paid by addressee

11711 N. College
Carmel, IN 46032

BUSINESS REPLY MAIL
First Class Permit No. 9918   Indianapolis, IN

Postage will be paid by addressee

11711 N. College
Carmel, IN 46032